Best
TEA SHOP WALKS
in
NORTHUMBRIA

Stephen Rickerby

Published by Sigma Leisure – an imprint of
Sigma Press, 1 South Oak Lane, Wilmslow, Cheshire SK9 6AR, England.

British Library Cataloguing in Publication Data
A CIP record for this book is available from the British Library.

ISBN: 1-85058-652-7

Typesetting and Design by: Sigma Press, Wilmslow, Cheshire.

Cover: Country Style Bakery tea shop, Middleton in Teesdale (Walk 20)

Maps and photographs:

Printed by: MFP Design and Print

Disclaimer: the information in this book is given in good faith and is believed to be correct at the time of publication. No responsibility is accepted by either the author or publisher for errors or omissions, or for any loss or injury howsoever caused. Only you can judge your own fitness, competence and experience.

Preface

Northumbria stretches from the Tees north to the Scottish border, including both Northumberland and Durham. There is a rich variety of landscapes in which to walk to and from tea shops – a variety, which the walks chosen for this book try to reflect. Scenery ranges from the dune-fringed coast of North Northumberland as at Bamburgh (Walk 3) to riverbank rambles inland as at Etal (Walk 1) and Yarm on Tees (Walk 21).

The North-East is, of course, equally rich in history and in industrial heritage. Walks in this book will allow you to sample this inheritance from the monastic relics of Holy Island and Durham (Walks 2 and 14) to the legacy of the Industrial Revolution as at Killhope Lead Mining Centre (Walk 7) and Allenheads (Walk 11).

Particular sites such as castles and cathedrals like Dunstanburgh, Warkworth and Durham (Walks 4,5 and 14) are also featured. Other interesting attractions include the afore mentioned Killhope Lead Mining Centre and the Washington Wildfowl Park (Walk 16). Sandy beaches add to the appeal of the walks at Bamburgh and Tynemouth (Walk 9), as well as being easily accessed from several other routes including the glorious Embleton Bay from the Craster and Dunstanburgh route.

Walking always necessitates a degree of forward planning and the walks begin with a thumb-nail description of the route to try to give you an idea of what the terrain and distance may entail, as well as, of course, what sort of tea you may expect to enjoy. This is intended to assist your planning, but you , of course, will still need to assess your aptitude to undertake a particular route, at a particular season and in particular weather conditions.

All the walks have been chosen because they are potentially interesting experiences and are not too demanding. The majority includes sections of cross-country walking, which require strong and sensible footwear. Sensible protection against the weather – rain or shine – is also a factor on a walk that may take you a mile or more from the nearest road or shop.

Maps are suggested for each walk. The Ordnance Survey Pathfinder and Leisure Maps are the best, and these are widely available in bookshops. Pathfinder maps are to be replaced by a new series of Explorer maps by 2002. In Northumbria, the Ordnance Survey plans to replace Pathfinders by Explorers by 2001.

Background information in differently styled print is intended to provide some interesting back up knowledge to enhance your enjoyment. Descriptions of the tea shops try to give a flavour of what to expect in terms of surroundings and fare. Where there is outside seating, this has been stated. Many establishments offer more than the tea-time treats described here – hot soups on cold, wet days for instance. For further details and to confirm opening hours, do telephone ahead where possible.

Acknowledgements

My thanks go as always to my wife Debbie and my daughter Katie for helping me on the walks.

Typestyle Conventions

To make the book easier to use, you'll find different styles of text:

Bold text to give directions.

Script-style, text for background information.
Enjoy your tea shop walks in Northumbria!

Stephen Rickerby

Contents

The Walks

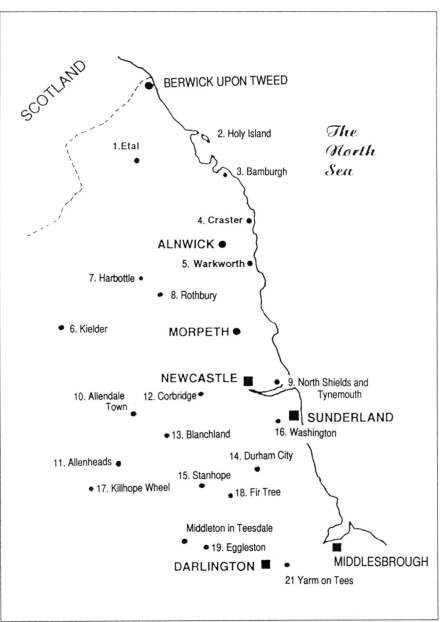

Location map (numbers refer to walks)

Northumbria

Northumbria is the Northeast of England, that is to say the region from the Tees to the Tweed – the old geographical counties of Northumberland and Durham, including the modern ones (still geographical counties despite being bereft of county councils) of Tyne and Wear and Cleveland. It is the region covered by the Northumbria Tourist Board.

The landscape

The upland rural fringe of Northumbria is the near continuous sweep of the North Pennines ("England's Last Wilderness") south of the Tyne Gap, mostly in County Durham, and the Cheviot Hills in the north-west of Northumberland.

The Cheviots are of volcanic origin and dominate the landscape structure of Northumberland. Their characteristic smooth, rounded profiles reflect their formation from cooled lavas which erupted nearly 400 million years ago and subsequently worn down by the combined actions of ice and weathering over the millennia. Views of the Cheviots are to be enjoyed on those walks in this book which are set in North Northumberland – for example, the two Coquetdale walks based on Harbottle (Walk 7) and Rothbury (Walk 8).

The North Pennines are only slightly younger, and are of Carboniferous age; they are a sandwich of sedimentary rocks – limestones, sandstones, shales and, on some summits, grit-stone capping. The key structural element is the Alston Block – defined by faults on three sides, this giant slab of rock tilts gently to the east beneath the Magnesian Limestone escarpment of eastern County Durham. The tectonic forces involved in such uplift and tilting led to the development of rich mineral ores in the Pennine region – lead, zinc and fluorspar among them. People were later to exploit these minerals and the remains of such ore mining are to be seen on upland walks in this book – Allenheads (Walk 11) and Middleton in Teesdale (Walk 20), for instance.

The Whin Sill is another magma-formed feature of special significance to the region's scenery. It forms craggy, near-vertical faces of resistant quartz dolerite leading to waterfall formation in Upper Teesdale and being taken advantage of for ancient fortification on the Northumberland coast, as at Bamburgh (Walk 3) and Dunstanburgh (Walk 4) Castles. The Farne Islands, visible from the beach between Seahouses and Bamburgh (Walk 3) are also made of Whin. The sill is hardened magma which, when molten, forced its way between deep strata to form a sheet beneath much of Northumbria. After solidification, it became exposed in a variety of locations because of the wearing-down of the land surface, standing proud due to its greater resistance to the forces of weathering and erosion.

In Northumberland, the Cheviots are succeeded to the south-east by escarpments of fell sandstone, as at Rothbury (Walk 8), interspersed by rivers such as the Till (Walk 1). Glacial activity included some erosion of upland valleys – the upper reaches of Coquetdale for example.

History

The history of the people of Northumberland – England's Border County – and County Durham – Land of the Prince Bishops – has been no less dramatic than the evolution of its physical landscape.

The border between England and Scotland caused frequent conflict to leave its mark on Northumberland especially. As far south as Blanchland (Walk 13) pele (or peel) towers were built as stone mini-castles to protect from the wrath of Border raiders. The example at Blanchland is incorporated into the Lord Crewe Arms – one of the tea taking possibilities described in the village.

Medieval County Durham was presided over by the bishops – the so-called Prince Bishops because of the earthly power they wielded. The seat of that power was at Durham City (Walk 14) on whose peninsula their castle and cathedral have stood since the 12th century. Durham Cathedral includes the shrine of St Cuthbert, one-time monk of Holy Island (Walk 2) and the Farnes (Walk 3) whose body was brought south by his followers and buried at Durham. This was supposedly on the advice of a local, when the wheels of the cart on which the saint's remains were being carried would turn no more.

The influence of the Prince Bishops extended to the very south of the County Palatine (as Durham County is otherwise known). At the dawn of the 15th century Bishop Skirlaw had laid the oldest stones still surviving in the bridge at Yarm on Tees (Walk 21). So, the life and legacy of Cuthbert may be seen to link the whole of Northumbria from north to south.

The North East has a rich industrial heritage. Walks in which some of this is revealed include Stanhope (Walk 13) and Middleton in Teesdale (Walk 20), as well as Tynemouth (Walk 9). Walk 17 (Killhope Lead Mining Centre) allows the opportunity to gain an insight into the life of the past recreated. Mining, steel and shipbuilding have given way to newer industries and services of the "New North East", typically at Washington New Town (Walk 16) where the Wildfowl Park forms the backdrop to the walk described here.

Natural History

The natural history of such a varied region is also wide in scope. The upland moors of Northumbria (as at Killhope, Walk 17, Middleton in Teesdale and Rothbury – Walks 20 and 8 respectively) is not truly wilderness. Like all English moorlands they are managed landscapes, the result of forest clearance and agricultural land use, mostly for sheep grazing. Bird life on the moors includes the golden plover, dunlin and birds of prey such as the Hen harrier, Peregrine and the elusive Merlin. Walk 6 at Kielder Water begins and ends at Leaplish where there is a Bird of Prey centre to visit. Owls are also spottable, particularly in County Durham and southern Northumberland. The heather moors are great insect attractors and butterflies and bees abound in summer and spring. Several of the featured tea shops sell local honey – for example, the Elm Tree House at Rothbury.

Northumbrian woodlands are home to starlings and great and blue tits, but also to less run-of-the-mill species such as the green and great spotted woodpeckers. Among the mammals, rabbits abound, and it will probably not be long before you see them while walking. Squirrels are commonly seen and deer may be spotted, for instance in the forest around Kielder Water (Walk 6). Otters exist in the rivers, but are difficult to spot, though mink are now quite wide-spread.

On the coast, dunes, as between Seahouses and Bamburgh (Walk 3) are stabilised by marram grass. In the slacks between the dunes orchids have been known, and among the grasses are pretty flowers such as burnet rose and bloody cranesbill. The crags of Whin Sill provide nesting sites for sea birds including kittiwakes and fulmars. In addition, puffins, guillemots, terns, shags and cormorants populate the bird sanctuary that is the Farne Islands.

People

Language, music, crafts and food are all aspects of the varied cultures of the region, part ancient rural inheritance, part customs of the great migrant workforce who arrived, mostly in the nineteenth century, to populate the industrial and mining villages and towns of County Durham and southern Northumberland.

The language of ancient Northumbria is Germanic, much more Anglo-Saxon in etymology as well as pronunciation, than the true English spoken further south. In many ways, it is not dissimilar to the Border Scots spoken north of the Tweed, and this linguistic continuity is reflected musically in the folk Border Ballads – songs whose themes, even words (give or take the odd place name) are indistinguishable north and south of the border.

"Geordie" like "Cockney" has a narrower strict definition than its common meaning. Strictly, a Geordie is born within sight of the Tyne – a less likely occurrence than in the past though still true of many people in North Shields for example (Walk 9). The dialect of the County Durham coalfield is "Pitmatic" – subtly different and with remnants betraying the Welsh and Scots roots of many mining families.

Ghosts proliferate. There are white ladies and grey ladies, nasties in coalmines like Blue Cap and Deugar, who reputedly throws walkers over cliffs – not many cliff walks in this book fortunately! The Lord Crewe Arms Hotel in Blanchland (Walk 13) has its own – Dorothy Forster.

Culinary traditions to whet the appetite include **Craster** kippers (Walk 4) and locally caught crab (Walks 2 and 4), Cotherstone cheese form Teesdale – look out for this in Middleton in Teesdale, Walk 20 and, of course stotty cakes, black pudding and singing hinnies – a kind of scone. Carlins are small hard peas, soaked in vinegar, which are still to be found on Carlin Sunday – the one before Palm Sunday in the run-up to Easter.

Tea Shops

The tea shops chosen are all cafes which serve the kind of fare one might expect at afternoon tea. The home-made cakes and scones they offer are described, though many have other food on sale – including hot meals as well. They vary considerably from small country tea shops – like the White Monk at Blanchland (Walk 13) to the lounges of grander hotels as at the Teesdale Hotel, Middleton (Walk 20) or Lord Crewe Arms Hotel also at Blanchland. Many offer the opportunity to sit outside to enjoy open views of the countryside like at Harbottle in Upper Coquetdale (Walk 7) or over lakes as at Washington Wildfowl Centre (Walk 16) or Leaplish, Kielder Water (Walk 6).

Some are in old, historic stone buildings like Vennels Café in Durham City, others like the two lakeside eateries at Washington and Leaplish are in modern wooden constructions. Others are parts of other facilities; the Restaurant at Yarm on Tees (Walk 21) is inside a small town department store and the Killhope Kitchen (Walk 17) inside the Lead Mining Centre at Killhope Wheel. Another tea shop with an industrial heritage theme is the Hemmel at Allenheads Heritage Centre (Walk 11). The Post Office Tea Shop at Etal (Walk 1) and the tea shop at Harbottle are both very much the focus of their tiny communities; others, such as Vennels in Durham City and the tea shops in Warkworth (Walk 5) and Holy Island (Walk 2) are more cosmopolitan in their wider part-tourist clientele.

Particular specialities are flagged up, especially where there is a Northumbrian slant to what is on offer. Examples which come to mind in this category are the Bark Pots at Craster (Walk 4) for crab, kipper and North Sea fish, Washington Wildfowl (Walk 16) for Pitman's stotty and a "Taste of the North" and of course the ubiquitous cheese scone. To a north-easterner such as myself the regionality of such a delightful, simple and seemingly commonplace item seems almost bizarre. Any tea shop will have cheese scones – if you haven't come across them before, now is your chance!

Paths

Long distance paths which cross the region include the Pennine Way from north to south and the Teesdale and Weardale Ways, which run from west to east. Sections of all these three are to be experienced on walks in this book. Parts of the Pennine Way are encountered on Walks 17 (Killhope) and 20 (Middleton in Teesdale) for instance and the Teesdale Way on Walk 21, Yarm on Tees. The Weardale Way is not confined to Weardale itself and parts of that long distance route crop up on the Fir Tree walk (no. 18) as well as the Washington route (Walk 16).

The Walks

Walks are chosen to be generally 2 to 5 miles long, circular and not too demanding. Where extra length of climbing of slopes is involved I have tried to flag the fact up. The walks reflect the varied landscape and heritage of Northumbria and stretch from the River Tees in the south to far North Northumberland – "The Secret Kingdom". Coastal walks include beaches at Bamburgh (Walk 3) and Tynemouth (Walk 9), as well as the dramatic Craster to Dunstanburgh Castle (Walk 4). Other historic backdrops exist to walks like the one snaking round the streets and incised meander river banks of Durham City (Walk 14) and the smaller, similarly sited (in a meander) Warkworth (Walk 5). Yarm on Tees is, of course, also nearly enclosed by a river loop – in this case the Tees. The walk here has riverside stretches, as do those at Etal (Walk 1) Allendale Town (Walk 10). The latter is one of the longest walks. It is possible to short-cut the longer walks – in the case of Allendale Town at Cattonlea Haughs and the directions attempt to give you pointers. Equally you may wish, as at Washington (Walk 16) to extend the route described, and advice is similarly available in the directions.

Tea shops are the bases for all the walks and these are nearly always in villages and towns – so nearly always on valley bottoms. For those seeking the open moors and heights options do, however, exist. Allenheads (Walk 11) claims to be the highest village in England. The Killhope Kitchen in Killhope Lead Mining Centre offers quick access to high moorland and stretches of the Middleton in Teesdale and Rothbury walks do too (nos. 20 and 8 respectively).

The majority of the walks are in the countryside and, although they are not serious hikes, sensible clothing and footwear have to be recommended. The weather can change suddenly and the going underfoot on surface country paths can often be sticky and muddy – "clarty" in the vernacular. Maps are provided in the book, but it is better to have your own OS map with you – available from good bookshops. Guidance is given as to which map or maps you may need. A particularly useful sheet is the OS Leisure Map 31 of Teesdale, which also covers Weardale.

1. Etal

Distance: 2½ miles.

How to get there: Etal lies on the B6354 between Ford and Duddo, 10 miles or so to the south-west of Berwick upon Tweed. It is well sign-posted locally.

Start: Etal Castle car park (GR NT925394,) OS Pathfinder maps 451 Norham and 463 Coldstream.

Etal is a chocolate-box pretty village of idyllic cottages, some thatched, stretched along its single street from the Manor to the ruined Castle. Etal, pronounced "Eetle" (like beetle, but with a silent b) is the most northerly village in this book – and the closest to Scotland which, as the crow flies, is only 4 miles to the west.

Etal Castle ruins with museum and the steam railway to Heatherslaw are the principal attractions for children. The gardens of the Manor are open to the public only on advertised fund-raising days. The Castle is open from Easter to October. Its museum includes an exhibition telling the story of the Battle of Flodden (1513). The entrance is through the car park and round the back of the unruined building, which houses the exhibition – sign-posted to the Railway. The railway has a halt at Etal from which you can catch the little train to Heatherslaw. The Castle was built in the 14th century.

The Tea Shop

Etal Post Office Tea shop is on the village street. It is open from Easter to 30th September from 10am until 4.30pm, though Wednesday and Saturday are half-days and the tea shop is closed on Sundays. All cakes, including carrot cake, gingerbread and date and walnut loaf and scones are home-made. There are daily specials on the board. Outside is a garden with patio tables on the lawn. Alternatively, if you take the steam train ride, there is Heatherslaw Corn Mill's Granary Café, which is open from 10am to 5.30pm during the same season as Etal Post Office, but is also open in October from 11am to 4pm (tel: 01890 820592). Tel: 01890 820220.

The Walk

Apart from the village itself, and some of the return along metalled lane, the terrain is mostly unsurfaced field and woodland paths. There are no especially steep slopes on this circular route from the village, along the bank of the River Till, through the woods and back over fields and along quiet lanes.

1. Start from the car park next to the Castle. Walk up the drive towards the main street, but turn left when you reach the end of the drive and walk, as sign-posted, towards the river. Go down the lane to the river's edge where there is a ford. However, you should not cross this. Instead, turn right and walk along to the end of the old footbridge. Do not cross this either! Turn right again and walk up the short flight of steps to join the footpath, heading left, parallel to the River Till. Keep going along the riverbank.

2. Reaching some ruins adjacent to a weir on your left, you will find yourself joining a wider track..

We are now at Barleymill Bank. The weir in the river would have helped to build up speed in the river to drive the mill's water wheel in the past.

3. Bear left along this track to reach a stile and gate combination. Negotiate these and continue along the path, passing by another footbridge. Keep going, through the trees, until you approach a leftward sweep of the river.

Keep your eyes peeled now. We are looking for a large horse chestnut (conker) tree on our right. Next to it there should be a conifer, with a path between the two.

4. Turn right onto the path between the two trees. Walk up behind the horse chestnut to cross a waymarked stile.

You will need to look carefully. If you have begun to follow the river leftwards, you have gone too far. At the same time, avoid being tempted by an earlier gully next to a narrow tributary and two

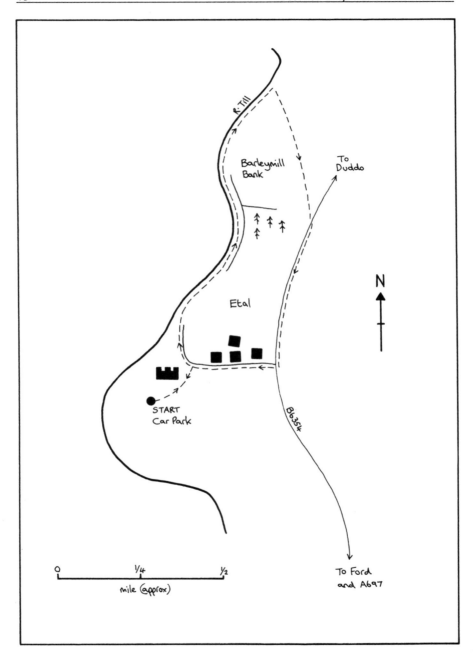

R. Till

Barleymill
Bank

To
Duddo

Etal

N

START
Car Park

B6354

0   ¼   ½
      mile (approx)

To Ford
and A697

tiny wood-fenced enclosures. The waymarking on the stile will confirm you are on course.

5. Walk up the gully beyond the stile and bear right at its end. Opposite you should see a conifer plantation and, as you scan left, a clutch of three and then two lone deciduous trees. In the gap is waymarked gate. Make for this target, and then, on the other side, follow the path straight-ahead across the pasture.

The hills you can see over to the right are the Cheviots. These hills are quite distinctive because of their rounded shape. This is because they are made of rock which is volcanic in origin.

6. The path ends at a stile. Cross it and walk to the right alongside the metalled road and return to Etal — at the opposite end of the village from the Castle.

As you walk along there are views over to the Till on your right, and you may be able to spot buildings you past on the early part of the walk.

7. Turn right and walk along the village street to the Castle car park.

Heatherslaw Mill

2. Holy Island

Distance: 3½ miles.

How to get there: Holy Island is accessed via a causeway from the mainland near Beal. Turn off the A1 between Fenwick and Haggerston Castle in north Northumberland, between Alnwick and Berwick upon Tweed.

Start: The car park just outside Holy Island village (NU 127422), OS Pathfinder 452 Beal/Holy Island.

Holy Island is so called because of its Benedictine monastery – now in ruins. It is the largest of the Farne Islands off the Northumberland coast – its alternative name is Lindisfarne. The island is connected to the mainland by a causeway that is only open when the tide is quite low. You will need to check the tide times in advance of setting

The Stables Coffee Shop, Holy Island

out – remember to also check for your return. Tourist information centres such as the one at Seahouses can help (tel: 01665 720885). The Museum of Island Life is open between Easter and October; it recreates the way of life of a fishing family living in and working from 18th century Hillcroft Cottage. For details telephone its sister facility – the Seahouses Marine Life and Fishing Centre on 01665 721257 or 720712.

The Tea Shop

The Stables, Holy Island is in the village. Walk from the car park to the central crossroads and you will find the Stables along the street to your right. Open from Easter to the end of September, from 10am to 5.30pm, though with variations for the tides at quiet times, the Stables offers plain, fruit or cheese scones with jam and butter or cream, toasted teacakes and filled rolls, including local crab. Apple flan, gateau and blackcurrant cheesecake are always available. Coffee is Mysore rich blend and tea Brodie's with Assam, Darjeeling, Earl Grey and Lapsang Souchong options. Tel: 01289 389325.

The Walk

The walk is a circular one around about half of the island, taking in the main sights of the Priory ruins, the harbour and the castle along the way.

1. Turn left out of the car park exit and walk down to the T-junction. Turn right and then left to walk straight on to the church grounds.

This is an opportunity to visit the Priory remains. There was first a monastery here in the 7 century. Monks who came from Iona, off the west of Scotland, founded it. However, this first monastery was built from wood. The stone ruins of today date from around 1000 AD.

2. From the ruins head back to the church. Turn left and follow the path to a single gate. Pass through it and turn left to walk along the track. At the end, head up the path to your left.

This ridge of rock is called a dyke. It protrudes due to the greater resistance of its igneous rock – solidified underground in the geological past.

3. Where there is a lower section to the ridge, bear left and then walk to your right along the gravel path.

The harbour here has traditionally been used by boats involved in catching crab and lobster. Crab sandwiches are a Holy Island speciality.

4. At the junction of tracks, turn right.

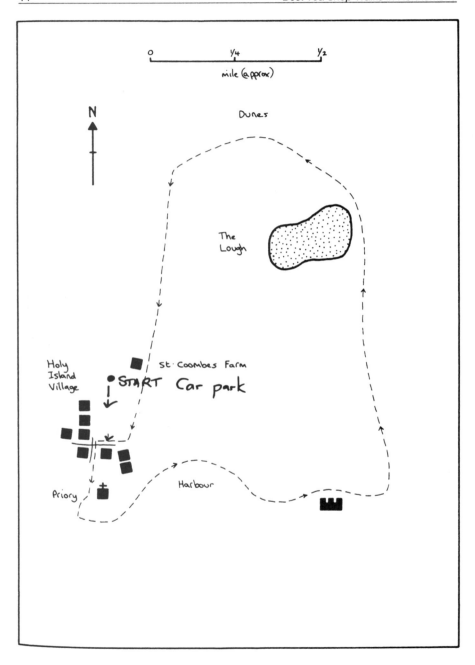

Ahead is the 16" century castle. This is rather recent as Northumberland castles are concerned. By then the monastery was closed and the island had become more significant for its role in the defence of the mainland, or rather to stop any potential invaders from using it as a base.

5. Pass through a kissing gate and bear left to walk around the bottom of the castle mount. Keep following the path as it swings leftward. Pass through another kissing gate and walk on to a junction of tracks.

A possible short cut from here is to turn left along the lane to return to Holy Island village.

6. Carry straight on.

The freshwater lake on the left is the Lough.

7. Walk on, to cross over a stile and then pass through a kissing gate before sweeping left over the more open country between the gate and the dunes. Walk along the near edge of the dunes until a path crosses your way. Turn left to join a clearer track. Follow this and return to the village.

3. Bamburgh

Distance: 5 miles.

How to get there: Bamburgh is on the dune-lined Northumberland coast, about 3 miles north of Seahouses. From the A1 you can drive to Bamburgh along the B1342 from Belford crossroads or B1341via Adderstone. The drive from Alnwick along the B1340 is the scenic route taking in Beadnell and some of the coastline en-route.

Start: Bamburgh car park (GR NU 184349), OS Pathfinder 465 Belford, Seahouses and Farne Islands

---

Bamburgh is on the north Northumberland coast, nestling with its green in the shade of an imposing castle. A fortification has stood on this prominent site since the 6th century. In those days, Bamburgh was the capital of the ancient kingdom of Bernicia and later site of the coronations of the Kings of Northumbria. The present castle dates from Norman times, although it was substantially remodelled

Bamburgh Castle

in the 19ᵗʰ century. It is open to the public and includes the Armstrong industrial heritage museum. Tel: (01668) 2142515. In the village itself there is also the Grace Darling Museum – dedicated to the heroine who saved sailors from the wreck of the Forfarshire off the Farne Islands in 1838. There is, however, no telephone.

The Tea Shop

The Copper Kettle tea room is on the village green, about halfway along on the left-hand side as you walk away from the castle. A founder member of the Tea Council's Guild of Tea Shops, it opens at 10.30am from March to October, closing at 5.30pm from May to September and otherwise half an hour earlier. The Copper Kettle opens some weekends in November and December – it is advisable to ring to check.

There is a large selection of teas and coffees on offer, and tea-time fare includes chocolate cake, banoffee pie, fruit cake, tiffin, flapjack, caramel shortbread, scones, tea loaf, cherry madeira and gingerbread. Outside is a patio garden. Tel: 01668 214315.

The Walk

The walk is across sandy beach on the way out, field paths and lanes on the more inland return leg. There is the option of an extension to visit Seahouses with its harbour and boat trips to the Farne Islands if you wish.

1. Start by walking out of the front of the car park and turning left towards the village.

To visit the village, simply turn left at the corner.

2. To follow this route, turn right at the corner of the road, onto the path which skirts the cricket field. Make for the base of the castle rock and follow the sandy path onto the beach. Turn right and keep walking.

Look out for these places on the beach walk: Bamburgh Castle, the folded rock strata of Greenhill rocks and later the stone beachside cottages at Monks House. As you walk down the beach you will, at low tide, have a wide expanse at your dis-

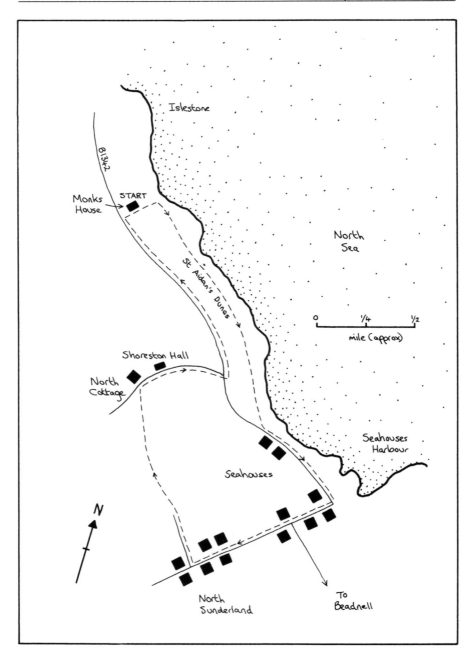

posal. At times of higher water, you may be more confined, possibly to the edge of the dunes themselves. In either event, you should enjoy a fine view of the Farne Islands which, although they may not look it, are some 1½ miles offshore. These islands are a bird sanctuary now but in the past were used by hermits, including St. Cuthbert for a time. In the other direction, at least from the top of the dunes themselves, you can see as far as the Cheviots, on a clear day.

There are boat trips to and around the Farnes from Seahouses harbour which you will reach later on the walk. The dunes you pass on your right, as you approach Seahouses, are St Aidan's Dunes.

3. Passing St. Aidan's Dunes, you will come to the end of the beach walk. At the end, ascend a flight of steps up onto the links.

To extend the walk by visiting Seahouses, turn left and walk along the top of the sea banks.

4. Turn right alongside the road and walk past the end of the houses. Beyond the first road junction, walk straight ahead on the landward side of the dunes. At the second, turn left and walk up the lane.

The walled grounds here are those of Shoreston Hall.

5. Beyond the Hall, turn right down a minor lane to pass South and North Cottages. Walk straight ahead until, having rounded a left-hand corner, you pass a ruin of on your left.

This is Saddleshall.

6. Beyond Saddleshall, go around two successive right-angled, right-hand corners to approach Fowberry. At the junction of lanes, turn right. Pass through the metal farm gate you reach and walk on to the next. Beyond it, walk along with the hedge on your left and turn right at the corner. Walk along the track, downwards, to another gate. Pass through and make your way up, along the path, to a wall ahead and a little over to your right. Follow the line of this wall onto a track, which takes you beyond the end of a lane on your right.

This is the lane leading to Greenhill Farm.

7.   Keep on this track, over field boundaries on the way, until you approach the stone-built house of Red Barns. Walk along the front of the house and through the waymarked gate at the end. Continue the few yards to the intersection of tracks and then turn left to walk up to a stile on your right. Cross and walk up to, and along the front of, the cottages. Beyond the cottages, proceed to the top of the mound in the pasture ahead. Follow the path diagonally down to cross the stile onto the roadside. Turn left to walk alongside the road to return to Bamburgh car park and around the corner and into the village to reach the Copper Kettle.

4. Craster and Dunstanburgh Castle

Distance: 3 miles.

How to get there: The Northumberland fishing village of Craster lies 6 miles to the east of the A1. From Alnwick follow signposts to Seahouses initially and then to Craster and Dunstanburgh Castle.

Start: Craster Tourist Information Office (NU 246198), OS Pathfinder 477 Embleton and Alnmouth.

Around the Tourist Information Office and its car park are a number of displays about the local heritage. You may think it a good idea to look at these before setting out. Craster used to be more than just a fishing village. There used to be fish and "chips"! The chips were pieces of ground Whinstone which was quarried here for use as roadstone. The Whin chips were taken down to the harbour and

Craster harbour

loaded onto ships there. When you reach the harbour you will be able to see the remains of the loading gear.

Adjacent to the car park is the Arnold Memorial Nature Reserve – one of 60 run by the Northumberland Wildlife Trust. You may want to explore this (admission is free) on your return from the walk.

The Tea Shop

The Bark Pots Tea Room in West End, Craster lies between the harbour and the Tourist Information Office. The name derives from pots found nearby. The bark of oak or elm was used to make a preservative in which fishing nets were soaked to prevent rot. There are scones to be had and a selection of home-made cakes. Toasted teacakes are another possibility and sandwiches include local fresh crab and smoked salmon. Hot dishes with a local flavour include Northumbrian fish pie and kipper crumblie. A range of teas, including herbal infusions, is available, as well as speciality coffees. Opening hours in summer are 8.30am to 6pm and in spring and autumn from 9am to 4pm. During January and early February the tea shop has weekend opening only. There is some outside seating. Tel: 01665 576286.

The Walk

This walk will allow you to explore the village and harbour at Craster before wandering along the shore to the ruins, returning across the fields. The ruined castle of Dunstanburgh is set dramatically on the rocky shore just over a mile from the village and can be reached only on foot. The ruins at Dunstanburgh are managed by English Heritage and are open to the public (tel: 01665 576231). There is a charge. The walk is mostly on unsurfaced paths, muddy after wet weather, adjacent to the rocky shore and then over pastureland and finally, briefly, through woodland.

1. Turn right from the car park exit and walk alongside the metalled lane into Craster village. You will pass the Bark Pots tea shop on the way.

2. At the harbour, turn left along Dunstanburgh Road.

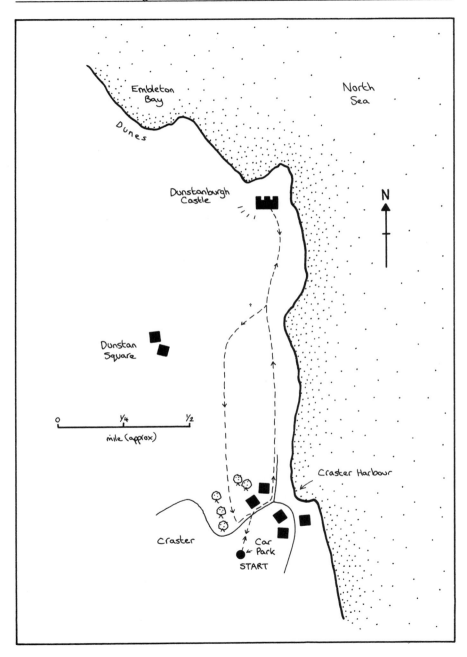

You may want to explore the harbour. The quays are accessible and the left-hand one has a plaque about the building of the harbour in 1906. At the end of the other is a squarish arch. This was the base for the loading gear used to pour the Whin chips into the holds of coasters.

3. Pass through the gate and follow the main coastal path all the way to the castle gates.

Dunstanburgh Castle was built over 600 years ago. During the Wars of the Roses it was a Lancastrian (red rose) stronghold, eventually over-run by the white rose Yorkists. As you climb the castle mound you will be able to see the glorious sandy beach and dunes of Embleton Bay beyond. To visit this, follow the path to the left of the mound or drive to Embleton after you have finished the walk.

4. From the castle, head back down to the fenced fields. Go through the first gate and then head diagonally up to the right.

The right of way shown on the OS map would have you walk as far as the next fence and then turn a right angle to climb the slope. However, it is clear on the ground that the diagonal route is the one people use and it does bring you to a stile. This is all National Trust land.

5. Cross the stile at the top and walk along the track until it dips down. At the bottom, turn left through a kissing gate and walk along the base of the cliffs on your left.

These cliffs are as rugged as they are because of the quarrying which went on in Craster until the 1930s. This particular stretch is called Dunstanburgh Heughs. Heugh is a local dialect word for rocky hill.

6. The path will bring you to a waymarked gate. Pass through it, and walk through the woods to return to the car park.

5. Warkworth

Distance: 2¼ miles.

How to get there: Warkworth is on the A1068 between Ashington and Alnwick. From the A1 turn east on the B6345 via Felton, or else on a minor road from Newton on the Moor.

Start: Warkworth market cross (NU 246061), OS Pathfinder 501 Amble and Lynemouth.

The small historic town of Warkworth is virtually enclosed by a meander of the River Coquet. It consists essentially of a single "bailey" street, which runs down from the castle at the top to the square at the bottom. Warkworth Castle is a prominent baronial fortification of 12th century vintage, home to the aristocratic Percy family until the 16th century.

Warkworth Bridge

The Tea Shop

There are plenty of places to choose from in Warkworth. Two, which are close together in Bridge Street, are the Castle House Tea Room, which has a patio outside and is licensed and the Courtyard Café, which has a varied choice of scones.

The Walk

Beginning from the market square, the walk takes you along the pretty banks of the Coquet, returning across fields to the castle itself and back to the market square via a narrow medieval lane. It is an easy route, rich in history.

1. Start from the market cross with the Masons Arms behind you. Head left, alongside the road, towards the Coquet, passing the Black Bull Hotel on your left.

Approaching the Coquet, there is a stone arch leading through to the old pack horse stone bridge. Inside the arch is a plaque about the 14" century bridge, which carried all the traffic in and out of Warkworth for over 600 years – until 1965 when the modern road bridge was opened.

2. Before reaching the old stone arch, turn left to follow the riverside path, signposted Mill Walk. Keep going until you reach a waymark sign at the end of Hotspur Lane.

3. Walk straight ahead along the now unsurfaced riverside path of Mill Walk in the direction of Howlet Hall.

You will pass Howlet Hall on the way to the castle. Walking round this meander one can see how the outer bank is steeper than the inner. This is because the river current has greater force there and can wear the bank away to form a river cliff. On the inside of the bend is a muddy beach, deposited by the slower current. This is the slip off slope. There are plenty of seats along this stretch. As you round the meander look behind for an excellent photo opportunity of the castle ramparts towering above the Coquet. Warkworth Castle was built 800 years ago. It was home to the Percy family – the Dukes of Northumberland.

4. When you reach a public footpath signposted to Warkworth Castle, on your left, ignore it and carry straight on.

A possible short-cut from here is to take the path up to the Castle and return to the market square from there.

5. On reaching a single wooden gate, pass straight through. Keep walking by the riverside until you come opposite Warkworth Hermitage.

In summer (from Easter to September) you can take the rowing boat ferry over the Coquet to visit this English Heritage site. A chapel was hewn from the rock here 600 years ago. The last hermit was George Lancaster who lived here in the 16" century.

6. Turn left, up the surfaced lane, away from the river. Keep going until you reach the stone cottage, which is Howlet Hall at the top of the rise. Pass through the gate and bear left at the T-junction of lanes. Keep going until you come to Crossroads Cottage.

Look into the garden of the cottage. The shelter is a boat!

7. Opposite Crossroad Cottage is a signposted public footpath leading to Warkworth Castle. Turn left along this field-edge path.

Looking ahead you should now be able to see the Castle.

8. Another path joins the route from the right. Carry on, bearing slightly left along the field edge towards the ruins and a wooden gate. Follow the path beyond, across the pasture, bearing slightly left again, and continue in similar fashion until you access the grounds of the castle itself.

As you near the castle, look down to the river and see if you can spot the path you walked along earlier. Ignore a path on your left, which leads back down to the river. The public right of way is through the grounds of the castle. To visit the castle, head

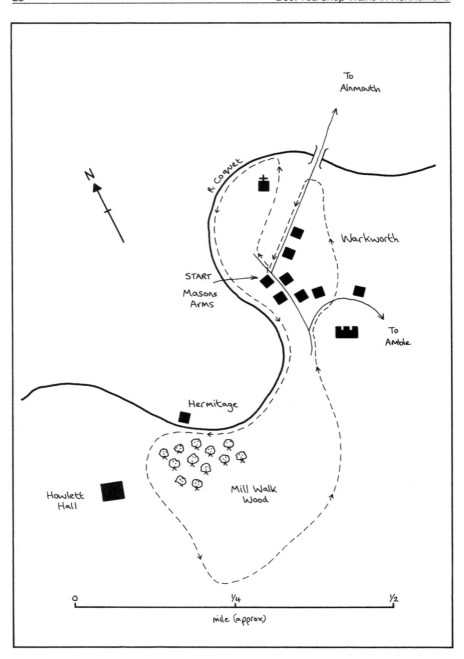

right to the bridge over the moat. It is open in the weekends, from Easter to September.

9. To continue the walk, follow the path to the left of the castle, descending stone steps into the moat.

Castles were, of course, often surrounded by moats which were filled with water to make them more difficult to attack. Drawbridges were used to facilitate access when there was no danger. The example at Warkworth is well preserved and one can allow one's imagination to run riot and conjure up images of the medieval past of this site.

10. Follow the path until you emerge from the grounds at the top of the main street.

As a short-cut, in bad weather maybe, simply walk down to the market square.

11. Turn right along Castle Terrace, crossing the street when it is safe—the bends and traffic volume here require a little prudence.

12. At the end of Castle Terrace is No. 5 which has a Shakespeare doorknocker. Turn left, hard by the side of the house, and follow the dogleg path right then left. Follow the long vennel (passageway) down to its end. This back lane is parallel to the main street of Warkworth. To either side are the long and narrow gardens of the houses. The lane has been here since at least the Middle Ages.

13. At the end of the narrow lane, turn left to the river end of the main street. Turn left up the street to return to the market square.

---

6. Kielder Water (Leaplish)

Distance: 2¼ miles.

How to get there: Leaplish Lodge Water Park is signposted from the road which skirts the western shore of Kielder Water between Stannersburn and Kielder itself. Kielder Water and Forest are signposted from main roads for many miles around — from, for instance, Otterburn on the A696 Newcastle to Jedburgh road, from the A68 Corbridge to Coldstream and the A69 Newcastle to Carlisle roads and from the nearby small town of Bellingham.

Start: Leaplish Lodge (NY 661878), OS Pathfinder 521 Kielder Water

---

Kielder Water is Europe's largest man-made lake. The reservoir has been landscaped and developed into an impressive scenic forest lake. Leaplish Water Park is one of several recreational developments on the shore. Facilities include an indoor swimming pool and sauna, boat hire and tuition, a children's play area, ferry cruising on Kielder Water and a bird of prey centre, as well as the Leaplish Lodge itself and, of course, walking.

The Tea Shop

Leaplish Lodge is a waterfront wooden cabin café. The ambience of Leaplish Water Park with its wooden single-storey buildings and co-niferous-clad hills surrounding the lake is rather North American. It is reminiscent of a Rocky Mountain location. It is open from Easter until the end of October from 10am to 5pm, later (until 11pm) in July and August and is also a licensed restaurant. Fare for tea-time includes home-made cakes and scones. There is outside seating and a panoramic view over Kielder Water. Ferry cruises leave from the adjacent jetty (for information, telephone 01434 240398) Tel: 01434 250312.

The Walk

This circular walk begins along the lakeshore and then loops back through the forest to Leaplish Water Park. Although much of the walk is on gravel path or metalled drive there are a couple of sections through quite rough grassland. Kielder Forest is a working forest. This has impacts on walking directions! Trees may be felled, previously felled clearings replanted and footpaths diverted. The guidance given here is effective at the time of writing but be prepared to be guided by any replacement waymarking which may be put in place.

1. Walk away from the Leaplish Lodge building and the lakeshore keeping the adjacent single-storey wooden building (housing the swimming pool among other facilities) on your left. Turn left onto the service road, across the culverted stream, and then left again onto the unsurfaced and signposted shoreline path.

Arriving at a line of coppiced beeches you should find an explanatory notice board to read. In essence these beeches are living relics of early enclosure which took place here at what was Mounces Farm in the 1770s. This is a good view and photo point.

2. Bear right to walk alongside the beeches on their landward side.

There is another path to the left of yours which you do not want.

3. Walk up the avenue, following, for the moment, the orange arrow trail posts.

In occasional beeches there are 'whirling beans' created by Northumberland artist Colin Rose. These are fibreglass spheres covered by coiled rope. Just beyond the informative notice board about these is such a beech (the third beyond the board) containing two whirling beans. This section of the walk is part of an Experiential Trail (leaflets about it are available at the Leaplish information office) and there are other sculptural devices you may spot – some musical. At the end of the avenue of beeches is a carved hedgehog.

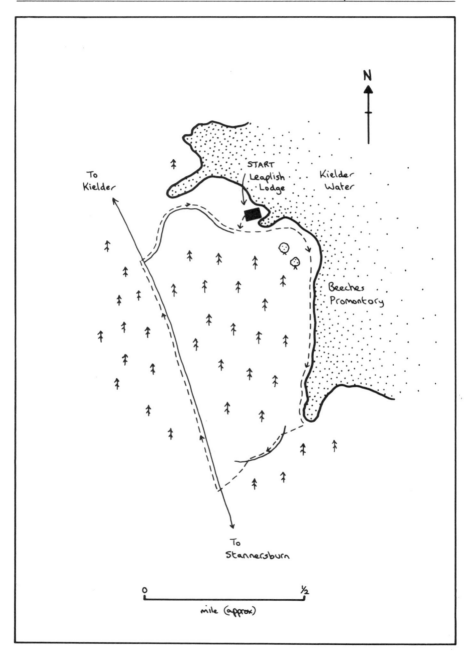

4. Just by the hedgehog, follow the orange trail marking as it directs you first right and then left. Arriving in a car park at the next inlet of the lake beyond Beeches Promontory where water skiing takes place, walk across to the wooden building. Follow the orange waymarking behind it, but keep your eyes open for the opportunity to rejoin the lakeshore itself. Pick up the gravelled shoreline public footpath again, using the more conventional yellow waymarking to help guide you now.

5. Continue to follow the shoreline path until where the lakeshore itself heads left along Bull Crag Peninsula the waymarked path takes you at right angles away from the shoreline.

At the next waymark post, there is a divide in the ways. It would be possible to turn left to continue along the shoreline path over a couple of footbridges, but this walk takes you straight on, away from the shore.

6. Walk away from the shore along the trodden path on the edge of the trees, up and away from the lake. Arriving at the service road by a waymark post, turn left along the road and walk on as far as the speed bump. Then bear left along the waymarked and initially gravelled path. Where the gravelled path takes a 90° left, head straight ahead along the rough grass path by the tree edge.

7. At the main road, turn right and walk on to the signposted entrance to Leaplish Water Park. Follow the access drive back to Leaplish Lodge.

7. Harbottle

Distance: 4½ miles.

How to get there: Harbottle is in the Upper Coquet Valley on the minor road from Rothbury (9 miles distant) to Alwinton.

Start: The Forest car park (NT 927047), OS Pathfinder map 499, Harbottle.

Harbottle is a small, linear village stertched along the minor road that wends its way along Upper Coquetdale between Rothbury and Alwinton. The earthwork remains of its 12th century castle – built to attempt to secure the area against Scots raids – lie behind the cottages of today's village.

The Tea Shop
The Coquet Crafts Tea Room in Harbottle is open daily from 10am to 5.30pm. Please check opening hours outside the Easter to end of Oc-

The Coquet tea room

tober season. Cakes and scones are all home-made and there is a choice of speciality teas. There is a large garden overlooking the village cricket ground and the Cheviot Hills where tea may be taken outside in good weather. The tea room itself is also the village shop and post office. There is a pets corner and children are welcome. Tel: 01669 650 348.

The Walk

This is a figure-of-eight route (see map) which enables you to do either loop as alternatives to the full walk. The first loop, around West Wood, to the Drake Stone and back involves something of a climb; the second across the Coquet and along track, lane and field path is more on the level.

1. Follow the track up the hill and past the Information Centre. Pass through the kissing gate and enter the Nature Reserve. Keep going uphill all the way to the top, bearing left to approach the Drake Stone.

2. Walk along the path to the right-hand bank of the lake – Harbottle Lough. Bear right, to walk along with the lake on your left as far as the fence.

3. Turn right and continue along with the fence on your left until you come into the West Wood. Walk straight on through the trees. Follow the line of the fence, downhill through the woods, until you reach a gate. Pass through and turn right onto the track beyond.

4. Coming to another gate, next to the Army Range signs walk down to the road, passing through two gates on the way.

    This is where the first loop of the walk can be brought to an end if you simply turn right and walk along the road to the car park. To keep going on the main walk, turn left.

5. Turn left onto the second loop. Walk along to and across the bridge over the River Coquet before turning right at the houses.

    This is Low Alwinton. Alwinton itself is a further half-mile up-valley.

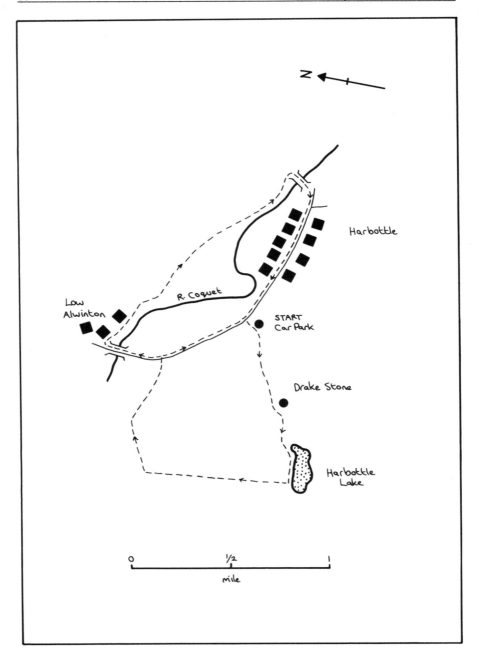

6. Follow the road and cross the cattle grids on the way up to Park House. Walk past the farm buildings on your right before passing through a gate and continuing upwards on the track beyond. Walk on, going through two further gates, before coming down to the trees of Ferny Wood.

7. After passing a lone cottage, cross the footbridge back to the south bank of the Coquet to Harbottle Castle. Turn right and walk into the village. Coquet Crafts Tea Room is along the street on your left.

The linear settlement of Harbottle is backed by the earthworks of its castle. These date from the 12" century when the fort was established by Henry II as headquarters for the Wardens of the Middle March – responsible for the security of this stretch of the English frontier with potentially hostile Scotland and Border raiders to the north. Destroyed on numerous occasions, only a single stone wall remains on the grassy mound now.

8. The car park is a further half mile or so beyond Harbottle, in the direction of Alwinton.

---

8. Rothbury

Distance: 3¼ miles.

How to get there: Rothbury is in Coquetdale. From the A1 take either the B6341 from Alnwick or, for a more southerly approach, the A697 Coldstream road just north of Morpeth, turning off for Rothbury north of Longhorsley.

Start: The Elm Tree House (NU 055017), OS Pathfinder 500, Rothbury and Felton

---

Rothbury is a thriving Northumbrian dales town, pleasantly sited on the north bank of the Coquet and acting as the principal settlement of Coquetdale. There is a wide range of shops where visitors can browse, and the grassy riverbank may be a good picnic site.

The Tea Shop

Elm Tree House is on Rothbury High Street. Its frontage is unprepossessing but the atmosphere authentically that of a north Northumbrian tea room. The market towns of the Borders – on either side of the Scotland-England divide – are characterised by such eateries. Not in the least twee, such places have long been venues for refreshment for rural locals, coming into the market town for the day, and travellers alike. Thus Elm Tree House is closely neighboured by, among others, the Sun Kitchen and the Turks Tea Room which is, typically, within the Turks Head public house.

In Elm Tree House, home-baking is the rule with a range of scones and cakes that includes such house specialities as cherry cheesecake, lemon meringue pie and pavlolas. There are two rooms. Upstairs there is table service and a view out across the green and over to the Simonside Hills. Downstairs service is at the counter. Also on sale, as well as home-made cakes, are honey and jams, and, at Christmas, puddings and Christmas cakes as well as shortbread and festive hampers. Tel: 01669 621337.

The Walk

From the old town of Rothbury, this route takes you up onto the heather moors above Coquetdale. The climb is quite steep, but once up on the moor the way is level and ends with a downhill route along tracks and lanes.

1.   Coming out of the front door of the Elm Tree House, turn left and walk down to Providence Lane. Turn left along it and walk up to the top.

There is a cul de sac of semi-detached houses slightly offset to the left ahead of you. Avoid the temptation to walk up this little street.

2.   From the end of Providence Lane turn left and walk along, passing Rothbury Antiques Store on your left, until you reach a row of detached bungalows on your right. Turn right up the footpath waymarked "Hillside Road ¼". When you reach Hillside Road turn right and then immediately 'left (effectively straight across), following the public footpath signposted to Cartington, up Blaeberry Hill.

3.   As the metalled lane swings left, the footpath takes you straight on to a stile. Cross onto the open moor and follow the series of waymark posts straight ahead.

Be careful on the heather moor not to confuse footpaths and watercourses. Initially you are heading straight ahead, up the slope. Check that you walking in a direct line away from the bungalow next to the stile. On your right, some metres away, is a plantation of coniferous trees. As the edge of these swings away to the right you should identify the next waymark post. From here the next waymark post is visible on the skyline.

4.   Keep following the series of posts up to and over the crest of the slope and through the boulder field until you are at a T-junction with a pebbly track. Turn left along this track and walk along as it swings left between the mast and the copse on Ships Crag.

Rounding Ship Crag, views over Upper Coquetdale and then of the rounded summits of the volcanic Cheviot Hills open up.

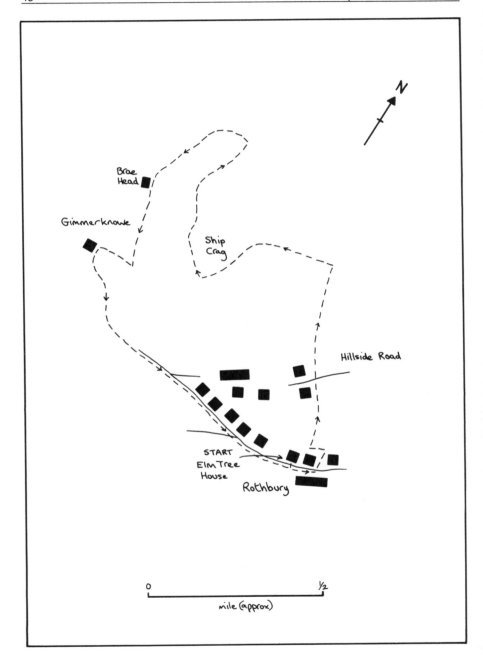

Brae
Head

Gimmerknowe

Ship
Crag

Hillside Road

START
Elm Tree
House

Rothbury

0   ½
mile (approx)

N

Rothbury Moor

Cheviot itself is the main hill of this range. In the geological past it was a volcano. Long since extinct, its lava flows have nevertheless had an effect on the modern landscape and are responsible for the smoothly rounded distinctive profile of the Cheviot Hills of today.

5. Continue along the track until, as it swings significantly rightward, you can see a drystone wall ahead, but downslope, to the left. An opportunity to follow a green track down to this wall soon arises. Take it. Set in the wall is a waymarked gate. Instead of passing through, turn left along the red track running along the face of the wall.

6. Simply follow the track. Pass the isolated though pretty stone cottage of Whinhams at Brae Head and keep going. The track will take you down into a dip and then part of the way up the other side. Here there is a waymarked gate. Turn right through it and walk along the track you join until you approach a cottage. This isolated homestead is Gimmerknowe.

7.   Turn left at the gate, without passing through it, and walk along the narrow grass trod, downwards to the trees. Follow the path as it sweeps left to follow the wood and wire fenced edge of the woodland. Cross the ladder stile you encounter and keep following the path ahead through the trees, bearing slightly right and downhill'

Through the trees you may be able to catch glimpses of the twisting River Coquet on its flood plain below. Following wet weather the water meadows to either side are often flooded and picking out the true river from the flooded creeks and pools is not that easy.

8.   The path becomes a narrow snicket between gardens and emerges onto the road via a steep and sudden stone ladder stile.

This stile comes upon you as a sudden drop. It is worth approaching it with care.

9.   Turn left along the road and keep following it back into Rothbury. When you do reach Rothbury House, bear left and you will return to the Elm Tree House.

9. Tynemouth

Distance: 4 miles.

How to get there: Tynemouth is of course at the mouth of the Tyne – on the northern bank. From Newcastle upon Tyne take the A1058 Coast Road and follow the Tynemouth signs. If you are travelling from the south use the Tyne Tunnel and then turn right onto the A1058 after initially following signposting for Morpeth and the North. Tynemouth is about 3 miles south of Whitley Bay.

Start: New Quay, North Shields (GR NZ 355678), OS Pathfinder 549 Newcastle upon Tyne and 536 Whitley Bay.

This walk begins by the River Tyne in North Shields and takes in the Fish Quay of that town as well as Tynemouth village (where the tea shop is located) and sea front where there are golden sandy beaches. Culminating in the former fishing village of Cullercoats, the route is unusually not completely circular on foot in that much of the return involves a short ride on the Tyneside Metro supertram system. If you prefer you can make use of that system to vary this walk. For example, you can park at Tynemouth and use the Metro to reach North Shields, or, alternatively, stop off at Tynemouth on your way back from Cullercoats.

The Tea Shop

The Studio Tea Room, Front Street, is a traditional tea room on the main street of Tynemouth village. Open from 10am to 4.30pm, the Studio, as befits the name, is surrounded by paintings for sale. This gives the feel of taking tea in an art gallery – though perhaps without the tense hush that may imply. There is a wide selection of scones including apple, apricot and hazelnut, pear and coconut. Home-made cakes change but may include carrot and orange or pear and chocolate. The view to the rear is over the garden towards the river.

The Walk

The walk is on surfaced paths for the most part, with a short grassy stretch by the Collingwood Monument and an optional beach section.

1. Start in the cobbled square of the New Quay.

From here you can look over the River Tyne to the town of South Shields. The ferry, which connects the two Shields, sails from the New Quay.

2. Walk past the Porthole pub.

Formerly the Golden Fleece, the PortHole was once notorious for all manner of dockside goings-on, including shanghaiing of sailors. The actual porthole in the door was taken from the Ark Royal.

3. Continue straight ahead along the flat road until you pass the Prince of Wales Tavern (old Wooden Dolly) on your right.

On the wall is a painted wooden doll. It is 8 feet high. Sailors used to cut a piece of wood from the doll before setting sail — to bring them good luck.

4. Keep walking to the Fish Quay itself.

The Fish Quay is where the once much larger North Shields fishing fleet lands its catch. There are numerous fish merchants all along here selling fish to customers and to shops all over the country.

5. Walk along the quay until you reach the covered section. Head to the left of this and look out for a stairway between the buildings on your left. Climb the stairs to the top and turn left along the river view walkway towards the white tower of the disused High Light.

The High Light and its twin on the quayside (the Low Light) used to be used to guide ships into the Tyne. Sea captains could line the lights up into a straight line — one behind the other and know they were steering a safe course into the river.

The Long Sands

There are some notoriously dangerous rocks (called the Black Middens) at the mouth of the Tyne. Sailors obviously wanted to steer clear of them.

6. Carry on past the High Light as far as Dockwray Square.

In the middle of the square is a statue of comedian Stan Laurel who was brought up here in Dockwray Square and before he moved to Hollywood when he grew up.

7. Retrace your steps along the river view walkway, but this time walk on as far as the Wooden Doll pub. Turn right and walk down this staircase to the quay. Turn left and then right, just in front of Dolphin Fisheries. Walk on to Clifford's Fort

This fort is named after Lord Clifford. It was built over 300 years ago and used for cannon which guarded the entrance to the Tyne.

8. Pass Clifford's Fort and turn left into the next yard of the Fish Market. Pass through this and turn right, keeping the herring smokeries on your right all the time, until you reach the path which leads on to the actual mouth of the Tyne.

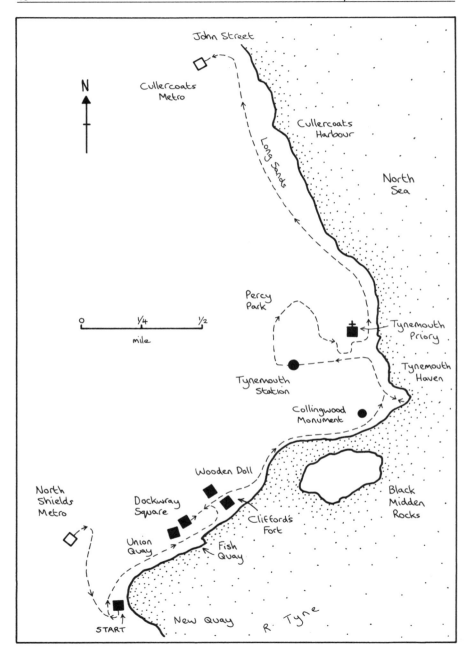

Herrings are smoked here over a slow-burning fire to make kippers.

9. Follow the waymarked path ahead in the direction of Tynemouth Priory and Castle.

The monument you can now see is to Admiral Lord Collingwood. Born in Newcastle in 1748 Collingwood served with Nelson at the Battle of Trafalgar in 1805. He is buried in St Paul's Cathedral in London.

10. Walk on along the riverside promenade until you take one of the paths which slope up leftwards to the Collingwood Monument. It doesn't matter which path you take – so long as it isn't the last one! You may let the children run on here, up to the Monument.

11. Walk to the right of the monument, and down the grassy slope beyond. At the bottom, take the path to your right as far as the access road to Tynemouth Haven. Turn right up to the vantage point, which overlooks it, and then return to the bottom of the dip where a path leads off right to the pier. Keep going straight ahead, up the hill, to the entrance to the Priory and Castle.

The headland has a commanding view over the Tyne's mouth and there have been fortifications here for as long as any one knows. The Priory itself has been here well over a thousand years – though it was rebuilt in the stones we now see before becoming ruined after the monastery was dissolved about 450 years ago. You may want to break off from your walk to visit this English Heritage site, or return by car after you have completed the route.

12. Turn left into Tynemouth village. Walk the length of Front Street, crossing the road at the end into Huntingdon Place and then bearing left to walk down to Tynemouth Station.

Tynemouth station is used by the Tyneside Metro now. However, the station itself is Victorian and has been recently restored. Look particularly at its glass roof.

13. Walk into the station and cross the footbridge to walk out the other side. Turn right up the lane and, at the end, cross the road, turning left, then right, past the nursery garden into Percy Park. Walk down Percy Park to the sea front.

A number of streets in Tynemouth are called Percy something or other. This one is Percy Park. Of marginal significance is the fact that this author used to live in Percy Park – at number 53. Percy is the family name of the Dukes of Northumberland who own much of the land on which Tynemouth is built. The triangular field here is called Sea Field. In days gone by it used to be used to graze cattle.

At the end of the street you will need to decide whether to walk down to the beach (the Long Sands) or stay on the path at the top of the Sea Banks.

14. Turn left and walk to Cullercoats.

The village of Cullercoats was originally much smaller and a fishing village. In Cullercoats is the Metro station where you can catch the train back to North Shields or just to Tynemouth. The old lifeboat station there is still recognisable - keep a look out for it. It is named and is at the corner of John Street.

15. From the harbour in Cullercoats, walk inland along John Street and then turn left down station Road to the Metro. Catch the tram (one every 10 minutes) to North Shields – two stops, or Tynemouth – just one.

If you break your journey at Tynemouth, walk out of the station without crossing the tracks and walk along the access road to Huntingdon Place. Continue in a straight line towards the village and the sea front. The Studio Tea Room is on your right just past the alternative No. 61 on Front Street. Alternatively, alight at North Shields and walk up to the station exit. Turn hard right to walk along the side of the station building until you reach Borough Road, third on the left. Walk down Borough Road to return to the New Quay.

10. Allendale Town

Distance: 7½ miles or 2¼ miles.

How to get there: Allendale Town is on the B6295 link between the A686 Haydon Bridge to Alston, and A689 Bishop Auckland to Alston roads.

Start: The Market Place, Allendale Town, NY 837558 (OS Pathfinder no. 560 Allendale Town and Blanchland).

Allendale Town is just exactly what it says – the town for Allendale. There are two Allendales – East and West – but the latter is relatively sparsely populated and does not support a town, so Allendale Town serves as the central settlement for both valleys. In the past, Allendale Town thrived as a centre for the old lead settlements of the twin valleys and its railway connections to the Tyne Valley, and thence to Newcastle upon Tyne, led to the early establishment of the tourist trade here. The market square is surrounded by rather fewer local shops than may have been the case in the past, but the Allendale Co-operative Society lives on, a survivor of the lead mining days of the last century.

The Tea Shop

The Allendale Tea Rooms are housed in an imposing listed, 18th century black and white building on the market square. There are home-made cakes, pies and scones. Opening hours are from 10am to 5pm, weekdays; 9.30am to 5pm on Saturday and 11am to 5pm on Sunday. The tea shop is closed on Mondays, except in the summer. There is a children's menu. Tel: 01434 683575.

The Walk

Leaving Allendale Town down the steep path to the river, the route takes you initially along the banks of the River East Allen and then across the fields to Catton, a village with a green ('green village' to geographers). From there the full route loops around over more fields

to cross the River Allen and return you to Allendale Town over farm-
land and lane. There is a shorter option described too – along the
East Allen to Cattonlea Haughs to cross over there and return over
fields and lane to Allendale Town.

The bridge at Allendale Town

1. Set off along the road signposted to Whitfield and Haltwhistle, so
that you leaves the square by walking cross the face of the Allendale Inn and then, in turn, the Hare and Hounds pub. Follow the
path which short-cuts the hairpin bend as you head down the
bank.

2. At the bottom of this little short-cut, cross the road to the
waymarked public footpath. The path is signposted to Allen Mill
(¾ mile) and Oakpool 2¾ miles).

3. Follow the path downward and along the bank of the East Allen.
Cross a footbridge beside a ruin.

The footbridge is over Philip Burn – a tributary of the East Allen. There are two Allens, East and West. West Allendale, on

the whole the wilder of the two, is beyond the watershed. The confluence of the East and West Allens to form the River Allen, a tributary in turn of the Tyne, is about 3 miles downstream of here.

4. Across the footbridge, bear left along the main path. Keep following the path through the wooded valley, sticking all the while to the main path wherever minor pathlets diverge. At a point where there are two kissing gates to your right, as the main path bends slightly leftward, continue on the main path and ignore the waymarked paths off to the right.

5. The riverside path emerges onto a metalled road beside a bridge over the river.

This is Cattonlea Haughs. To short-cut the walk and take the lesser distance option, cross the bridge and take the second path on the right (see direction 25).

6. Cross over the road but not the bridge and take the track straight ahead between the river and the row of cottages. Go along this waymarked track towards Catton and follow it as it curves right, with the river on your left, until it narrows to a path along the actual river bank. By the new sewage works, the path swings right to lead onto a metalled roadway. Carry on up this a little, ignoring a public footpath waymarker on the left, until you pass through the embankment of the dismantled railway.

7. Then, follow the waymarker left, over the stile, towards Catton. Walk straight down the dip to a marked corner of the fence and then, just beyond this, right, over a wooden footbridge, across a stream. On the other side, follow the path ahead as it bends slightly left up the rise and on as far as the top lefthand corner of the field. Cross the ladder stile here into the pasture beyond and walk around it, keeping the drystone wall on your left, towards a wooden gate. Pass through this waymarked gate to emerge between the houses onto Catton village green

The green village of Catton is named after the local wild cat, and its enclosed shape reputedly reflects its foundation by a

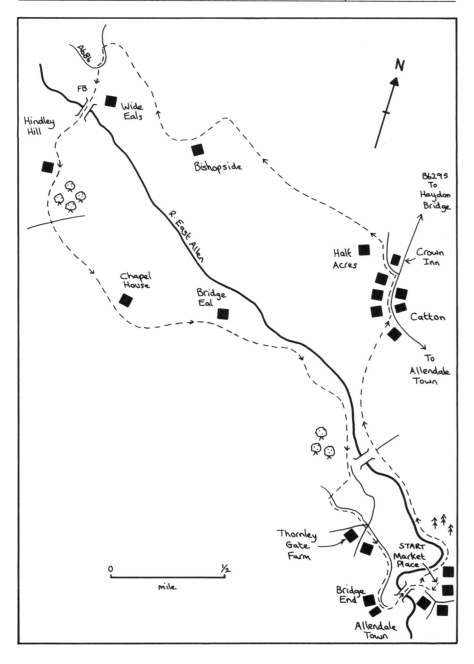

group of Saxons who retreated up the East Allen valley to es-
cape Viking raiders. They established their homes in a ring for
defensive purposes and to protect their livestock. This ring is
comparable to modern African kraals or to Wild West wagon
circles and it simply transferred itself down the ages as
homes were replaced — eventually by stone cottages.

8. Walk up the length of the green and a little beyond to the Crown
Inn. Turn left down the minor road signposted to Staward. Walk
down into the dip and up the other side to the left-hand bend. On
the bend is a public footpath sign, but ignore it and continue to a
second sign pointing left down the lane. The sign indicates the
way to Half Acres and Old Town.

9. Walk down the lane, keeping the drystone wall on your left. This
is the right-hand lane of two. At the right-hand bend in it, there is a
waymark stile to cross. Beyond it, head left, keeping the fence
and its succeeding drystone wall on your left, as you walk round
the edge of the pasture. Half-way round is an open gateway with
adjacent stone stile to negotiate before continuing in the same direction as previously, but with the drystone wall now on your
right. ·

10. At the field corner are some yellow waymarkings. Go straight
ahead and over a stone stile to continue along the side of the next
pasture, drystone wall on your left. Cross the next stone stile, and
carry straight on to the ladder stile ahead. Beyond this, walk
slightly right along the curving path — marked by a slight depression. After a little while you will see that you are apparently heading straight towards a house.

11. Persevering across the pasture, you will reach a drystone wall
corner. Continue straight ahead towards a telegraph pole, keeping the drystone wall on your right. Come to a stone stile and
cross it, carrying straight on with drystone wall on your right towards the next stone stile which you can already see because the
stones have been picked out with white paint. Cross this in turn
and keep going straight ahead to the evident signpost at the field
corner.

12. By the signpost, negotiate a wooden gate to come to a surfaced lane. Turn right and then immediately left round the right-angled bend of this lane. At the junction, carry on straight ahead, rather than turning right. At the next junction, again go straight ahead — along the minor lane.

13. Passing stone-built Kilnburn on your left, the stony lane dips down to a divide in the ways. Take the left-hand fork and, coming to a green metal gate, pass straight through it and carry on, with the drystone wall to your left, along the edge of the pasture. At the bottom of the field there are two exit gates to choose between. Opt for the left-hand, waymarked, red metal gate, and pass through it to dip down towards Bishopside.

14. Just before reaching the house at Bishopside, turn right through a waymarked green metal gate up to the corner of the fence. Turn left, as waymarked, with the barbed wire fence on your left. At the next corner in the fence is another waymark arrow — just carry straight on to the field corner where there is a stile to cross over onto the line of the dismantled railway. Just to your right is a ladder stile to cross so as to head diagonally right, across the field towards the midway point between two telegraph poles.

15. On the second telegraph pole — the one further down the slope — is a waymark arrow. Allow it to pint out another yellow waymark arrow on the field boundary a little up to the right. Make for this arrow and pass straight through the gate you find to walk along the grassy path to a drystone wall. Follow this wall on your left. The grass track leads down to a metal gate which admits you to an area of coniferous woodland. Follow the track ahead down to the main road.

16. Turn left, alongside the main A686, and walk downhill to the hairpin bend. However, you do not round this bend. Instead cross over and head along the track, which leads straight on, beside the sign for Wide Eals. Follow the lane down to a second gateway in the drystone wall by the farm itself. Turn right here and carry on along the front of the farm before turning left down the side to a wooden bridge which takes you diagonally right across the East Allen river.

17. On the other side of the bridge, carry on straight ahead towards the corner of the line of deciduous trees. There is a waymarked gate to pass through before rising slightly into a more open pasture. The grass path then heads diagonally left up the hill. Follow the path up the steep bank at the top of the field, to reach the fenceline. Turn left and follow the track which parallels the fence.

18. At Hindley Hill Farm, turn left at the first waymarked gate to make your way through the farmyard, keeping the main buildings to your right, and make your way to the track which runs along the right-hand side of the trees ahead. These are coniferous trees — not deciduous as your OS map may suggest.

19. Emerging at the minor road, turn initially right and walk uphill for just a few yards. Almost straight away, on your left, you should see a waymark post directing you across the fields in the direction of Chapel House. Pass through the gate into the pasture beyond and walk alongside the drystone wall on your right until you come to a waymarked ladder stile. Having crossed it, carry straight on along the edge of the next pasture with a drystone wall now on your left. At the end of this field, cross a ladder stile and turn left to follow the drystone wall round to the left and then to the right by a stone-built house.

20. Walking along a quite evident track towards Chapel House, you come to a gate. Cross the waymarked stile beside it and a very small triangular piece of ground. A second stile then leads you onto a lane. Walk along this a little way and you will find, in quick succession, two stiles across the wire fence to your left. Cross either into the pasture and walk diagonally over it to a waymark post in the opposite corner, by some trees.

21. Cross the stile beside the waymark post and follow the grass path on the other side. Where there is a slight divide in the way and a low drystone boundary curves left, take the leftward option. Follow a hedge, and then a fence, on your left to a waymarked wooden stile. Cross into the woods and carry on straight ahead to the riverside, crossing Maggy's Bridge over a tributary stream.

22. On the other side of the bridge turn left and follow the River East

Allen as far as a waymarked stile across the drystone wall on your right. Over this stile, you continue in the same direction, but now with the wall on your left.

23. At Bridge Eal, there is waymark guidance after you cross the little stream there. This directs you right, away from the stone-built cottage, between drystone wall to your right and fence to your left, to a second waymark at a stile. Cross this stile and turn sharp left to walk along the quite clear grass way alongside the wire fence. Carry on straight along this grass way where the wire fence reaches a corner.

24. Pass a footpath indicator, and just keep going straight ahead. Waymarking takes you beyond a gateway with a stile beside it into the next field. Follow the lane straight across the middle. The far side of this field is marked by a very low stone boundary between two trees, which form part of a line of deciduous trees. Crossing this boundary, the stonier lane bears slightly to the right. Carry straight on, across the grass to a waymarked stile beside a metal field gate. Cross this stile to the footpath beyond and, between two low trees, you should come to a drystone wall and the actual riverside.

25. Walk along with the River East Allen to your left, crossing a low hurdle stile on the way, to the end of the path at a kissing gate by the road bridge. Do not cross the bridge over the East Allen, but turn right. Ignore the first waymarked path on your right (signposted to Oakpool) and carry on to take the second, just past the entrance to Brideshill cottage. Walk along the path into a wooded glade. Beyond the glade, the path takes you over a stone stile into a pasture. Walk along the right-hand edge of the field to a ladder stile at the top end. Cross this and turn left along the metalled lane to walk on as far as a five-ways cross-roads.

26. At the cross-roads, carry straight on in the direction signposted Allendale. Follow the road down and around, to cross the bridge back into Allendale Town. Walk up the path to the market square.

11. Allenheads

Distance: 6½ miles.

How to get there: Allendale Town is on the B6295 link between the A686 Haydon Bridge to Alston, and A689 Bishop Auckland to Alston roads.

Start: From the front of the Heritage Centre (NY 859453), OS Pathfinder 570 and Rookhope.

Allenheads claims to be England's highest village. In 1985 it was depicted in the press as a dying village which provoked the local population to do something to save it, and the Allenheads Trust and Heritage Centre were born. The Allenheads Heritage Centre (tel: 01434 685395) is open daily, except at Christmas and New Year and during bad weather in winter, from 10am to 5pm. It is a community-owned heritage centre run by local people, which houses an exhibition and audio-visual show describing the history of this former lead mining village.

As well as the tea shop, there is a nature trail, picnic area, blacksmiths shop and the only known surviving hydraulic engine built by Lord Armstrong (in 1852).

The Tea Shop

The Hemmel Café is in the Allenheads Heritage Centre. Housed in a stone building fronting the attractive courtyard where there is outside patio seating, this café offers a variety of home-baked produce. The name Hemmel originates from the original purpose of the building as a byre or hemmel for Allenheads Farm. The Allenheads Heritage Centre is open from 10am to 5pm daily, except Christmas and New Year's Day. Tel: 01434 685 395.

The Walk

From Allenheads village, this walk takes you up onto the edge of the moors and then across rough pasture lands down the upper part of the East Allen Valley before returning you to Allenheads mostly though not entirely alongside the valley floor road.

1. Standing with your back to the Heritage Centre entrance, turn left along the B6295. You are walking in the direction signposted to the Methodist church. Keep going until, just before reaching a bridge over the river, you find two wooden footpath signs on your left. Follow the guidance given by the first of these and walk up alongside some stone cottages. At the end of these cottages, the track veers slightly left to take you behind an old barn before climbing further to a fork. Turn right across a small stone bridge and walk as afar as the metal gate across the driveway to a small stone cottage. Turn left, following waymarks, and walk along with a fence to your right and stream gully to the left.

2. Follow the line of the fence to a waymark post you can see ahead. Turn right, as indicated along the flat, grass way with a ditch down to your left. Where there are some television aerials on posts, it begins to run parallel to a drystone wall on your right. Keep going, following the wall around, until you begin to see a waymarked ladder stile ahead. Cross the stile and turn left to follow the drystone wall on your left, along the edge of an enclosed pasture. Keep following the wall until you come to the next waymarker post beside a stile.

3. Cross the stile and keep following the line of the wall to your left until you join the farm track. Walk along this, in the same direction as before, and round a right-hand bend to come to a waymarked gate. Leave the track and walk right of this gateway, along the field edge with the wood and wire fence on your left. Carry straight on to a small stone farm building, passing to the left of this. Follow the directions shown by a waymark arrow, and make straight for a ladder stile.

4. Having crossed the stile, continue straight ahead, passing the abandoned farmstead of Viewly Hall on your left.

    A number of abandoned farmsteads are visible from this point – testament to the precariousness of marginal farming here on the edge of the wilderness.

5. Follow the path as it dips through a gap in a broken drystone wall. Keeping the drystone wall on your left you come down to a further

ladder stile which you cross to veer a few yards down to the right to join the old grass farm track leading up to the abandoned farmstead behind you.

6. Follow the grass track round to the left at first and down to the stream, using the stones to help you across, before it leads you out onto the open moor. Keep going along the track towards the brow of the hill where there is a meeting of tracks. Head right down the major track that you have now joined.

7. Where the track curves left, cross the ditch to your right to the grass embankment on the other side. This is the right of way; follow it straight ahead down the slope – some stones mark part of the way. Head for the ruin at the slope foot and find the blue waymark arrow that guides you straight on. Then, drop down to your right, heading straight for a metal gate at the roadside. Pass through and turn left along the minor road, not crossing the bridge, and walk up the hill.

8. Pass the cottages at Slag Hill and drop down into the dip to cross Wainford Bridge to round the right-hand bend and go up the other side to reach a road junction. Turn right at this intersection and walk along the quiet tree-lined lane. Passing the buildings at Hammer Shields, ignore both the ladder stiles on your right and the signposted footpath to the left. Beyond the entrance to High Huntwell you begin to descend, following the lane round to the right and then to the left to reach the bank of the River East Allen.

9. Continue along the lane, tall trees to your left, past Breckonholme on the opposite bank, until you reach first a ford and then a footbridge. Cross neither, but proceed straight ahead along the waymarked riverside track in the direction of Spartylea. Keep going until you arrive at a gate beside a waymarked stile. Cross the latter into a meadow and carry straight on along the riverside until you come to a low stile over an equally low drystone wall. Proceed ahead, in the same waymarked direction, with small trees to your right, until another stone stile takes you over another wall. Keep on the waymarked river path, with the drystone wall of a churchyard now to your left.

10. Between the wall and the river is a wooden hurdle to cross before

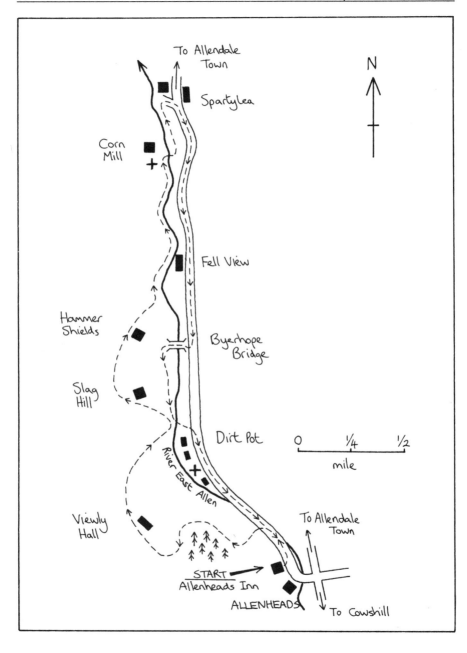

coming to the church itself. Turn right over the bridge and follow the way indicated by a guidepost on your left. Over the drystone wall, you cross a pasture where a little gully takes you down to a track and onto a footbridge over Ellershope Burn — a tributary of the East Allen. On the other side, follow the track straight ahead to the remains of an old stone enclosure, passing just to the left of this to continue across the pasture. Look out for a waymarked stile on the field boundary, just below a telegraph pole. Reaching it, cross over and walk straight across the middle of the pasture towards Spartylea.

11. At the end is a green metal gate to pass through. Resist the temptation to turn left through the white gate, but instead press straight ahead past an old stone building on your left and you will come through a gap in the fence to a set of cut steps with wooden handrail leading up to the roadside fence. Turn right along the lane and then right again along the main B6295 road.

12. Walk past the cottages at Ellershope Bridge, ignoring the lane leading down to Corn Mill and keep going until you pass White Hill on your left. As you approach the row of cottages at Fell View, ignore the road dipping down to the right, and carry along the straight section of the road ahead. Where the road takes a left and right bend in quick succession, a stone track leads down to the right from the first of the two. Go down this track, with the drystone wall to the right, past the gateway to the house on the right and then round to the right.

13. Walk down and a stream will appear on your left. This is Byerhope Burn. Follow the track around to the right and look for a gap in the drystone wall on your left which leads you to a cut down to a white metal footbridge, Use this to cross the East Allen and then turn left along the riverside path. Cross the tributary Middlehope Burn by another white footbridge and continue, following the riverside as far as the next bridge over the river — one you will recognise from earlier.

14. This time, turn left to cross the bridge before heading right, back to Allenheads.

12. Corbridge

Distance: 2½ miles.

How to get there: Corbridge is well signposted from either the A69 Newcastle to Carlisle or A68 Darlington to Edinburgh roads. There is parking in the village square.

Start: In the village square, by the market cross.

There are two market crosses in Corbridge. One dates from the 13th century and the other, the Percy Cross, was erected in the late 19th century by the then Duke of Northumberland. Percy is the family name of the Dukes of Northumberland. A plaque identifies this latter cross.

Watling House

The Tea Shop

Watling House is in the centre of Corbridge. From the market cross head past the church, keeping it on your right, and you will, in just a few paces, see the tea shop ahead of you. Specialities include home-made scones, soup and a range of home-made dishes as well as an assortment of cakes. Watling House is open from 10am to 5pm, Monday to Friday (5.30pm on Saturday) and on Sunday from 1.30 to 5.30pm.

Other tea shop options in Corbridge include Chadwicks, Middle Street and Gresham

House which has a "Secret Garden" to the rear where tea may be taken overlooking the Tyne. Tel: Watling House, 01434 633095.

The Walk

From the central square of Corbridge, this walk takes you across to the south bank of the Tyne for a gentle woodland stroll. Much of the walk is on well-trodden field and woodland paths or on quiet metalled lanes.

1. Begin at the market cross in the village centre. Walk along the length of Middle Street and turn right to walk down to and across the road bridge over the Tyne.

2. Having crossed the river, bear left towards the Lion of Corbridge hotel. Before reaching the hotel, take the signposted public footpath on the left.

   The sign is to Farnley Grange (1 mile). You will be walking past the walled grounds of this estate a little later.

3. Cross the stone slab stile and walk along the wooded riverbank path. The path divides and merges in a braided, anastomosing pattern as it guides you through the woods until it brings you to the end of the stone wall which has thus far been your companion on your right.

4. From the end of the wall, continue straight ahead along the now slightly wider woodland path.

   To your right now is Tynedale Park rugby ground.

5. Continue along the path until you have passed Tynedale Park, but keep your eyes peeled for a low waymark post set to the left of the path. Turn right to make your way over to a ladder stile beside the railway.

   This is the Newcastle-Carlisle line. Trains run along here quite frequently and you will need to heed the "Stop, Look, Listen" notice and cross the double track with care.

6. On the other side of the tracks, carry straight on up and over the

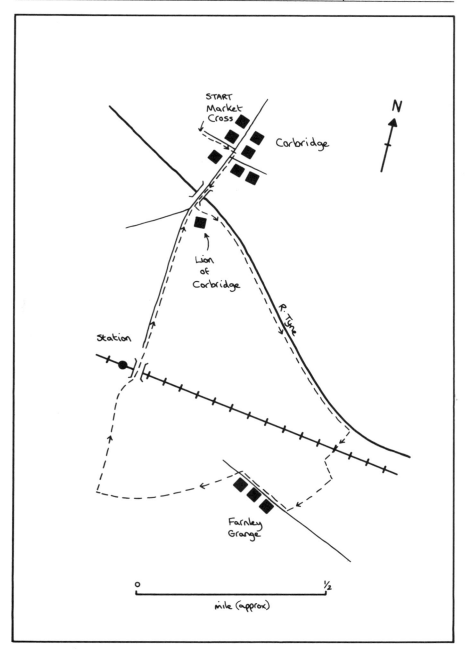

waymarked stile and on into and through the woods until you ascend a stepped section and reach a stile accessing a crop field. Cross the stile and turn right along the edge of the field, making for a single wooden gate set in the drystone wall ahead.

7. Pass through the gate and turn right along the path adjacent to the metalled road.

The grounds of Farnley Grange are on the left along this stretch and views across the Tyne valley and Corbridge village to your right.

8. Carry on beyond a row of ribbon development villas on the left, to turn left along a metalled lane signposted to Temperley Grange and Prospect Hill. After a few metres turn right along the signposted, metalled public footpath in the direction of Mount Pleasant and West Farm.

9. After you have passed the walled and gated grounds of Ravenstone and then the stone bungalow of Dunroamin, turn right across a stile (there is another on the left which you should ignore) to follow the field-edge path.

Corbridge is now clearly visible, straight ahead and there is fine vista of the Tyne Valley to enjoy.

10. The field-edge path terminates in a stile bringing you to the edge of a main road (the A 6080). Cross the road carefully to the waymarked stile directly opposite. Cross this stile and continue straight ahead along the edge of a pasture.

You will see the platform of Corbridge station ahead, at the bottom of the bank. You are not walking right down to it, however

11. Halfway down the bank is a kissing gate. Turn right through this into a wooded section of path. Follow the path to its end and turn left along side the metalled road to cross the bridge over the railway, next to Corbridge station.

The station allows commuters to travel easily into the business centre of Newcastle upon Tyne to the east. Corbridge is something of a gentrified settlement, with bijou shops whose

evident prosperity is to a considerable extent due to its links with that city.

The road you are now walking beside was the A68 in its time, but this section has been left quiet and isolated by re-routing of that trunk road. Thirty years and more ago Corbridge was a congested route centre where the A68 high road to Edinburgh crossed the A69 Newcastle-Carlisle cross-country route. The bridge itself, being single lane only, was a real bottleneck.

The presence in Corbridge of so many, some quite large, inns reflects its past as a major transport node, a role dating back to Roman times when Dere Street — the Roman road from York to Edinburgh crossed the Tyne here. The remains of the Roman town of Corstopitum lie to the north of modern Corbridge.

12. Cross the bridge, back to the north bank of the Tyne and walk back, along Middle Street, to the village centre.

13. Blanchland

Distance: 2½ miles

How to get there: Blanchland is on the B6306 Hexham to Carterway Heads road. The latter is on the A68 Darlington to Corbridge road, north of Castleside. Hexham lies just south of the A69 Newcastle upon Tyne to Carlisle trunk road.

Start: The car park in Blanchland

Blanchland lies on the north bank of the Derwent and thus qualifies – just – to be in Northumberland, whereas the nearby and picturesque Derwent Reservoir is in County Durham. Stone-built cottages surround the village square, which may be accessed at its northern end via a stone arch. Though something of a tourist honeypot in the

Blanchland

summer, Blachland is a sleepy place out of season, with only a couple of shops in addition to the tea room and the hotel.

The Tea Shop

The White Monk tea rooms are located behind the main square of Blanchland. From the bridge over the River Derwent head left instead of walking directly into the square and you will find the tea shop on your left. The White Monk is open daily from 10.30am to 5pm from June to September and at weekends from March to May and in October – again from 10.30am to 5pm. On sale are sandwiches, home-made scones including girdle scones and wholemeal, cakes such as cherry and almond, lemon drizzle and coffee and walnut and biscuits like flapjack and shortbread, as well as home-made jam and chutney. Set, traditional afternoon teas are the house speciality. Tel: 01434 675044

The Lord Crewe Arms Hotel also serves afternoon teas from 2.30 to 5.30pm. There are scones and home-made cakes including lemon and walnut, chocolate cake and coconut cake. There is outside seating available in the courtyard garden. Tel: 01434 675251

The Walk

The walk begins in Blanchland village and takes in a riverside outward leg followed by a return through coniferous forest.

1. Walk out of the car park entrance and turn right to walk to the square in the centre of the village, passing through the stone arch there.

    The enclosed square of tiny stone cottages is the heart of the village here. Beside the stone arch is the Post Office. This, with its flagged floor and traditional wooden counters, is a real throwback to Victorian times.

2. Walk through the square and on as far as the bridge over the River Derwent, but do not cross it. Instead turn left to join the riverside path which is accessed by turning hard right alongside the parapet until you come to the river bank itself. Turn left to walk along in the same direction as the Derwent is flowing.

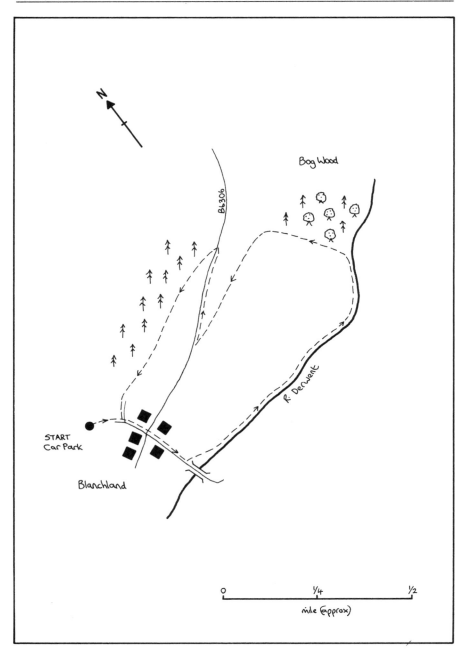

As you walk along here look out for wire cages on the banks. These are grabions. The stones encased in them are to protect the riverbank from erosion by the river. They are usually on the outside of river bends because this is where the force of the river is greater.

3. Keep going along the riverside path. On encountering a pair of ladder stiles, cross them both and keep walking by the river, crossing a broad area of grassland on the inside of a meander. At the waymark post, turn left along the drystone walled track and keep straight ahead until there is a right-angled corner, taking you leftward.

This flat area is the flood plain of the river. The land here would be wetter if it were not for the land drains that have been dug in the soil next to the path.

4. Walk on as far as the road. Turn right and walk uphill. Keep alongside the road until you enter the wood. Look out for a public footpath waymarker on your left. Turn left, almost back on yourself, to approach a waymarked seven-bar gate. Pass through and walk along the woodland track to a divide. Bear right.

5. As the woods clear, a track joins from the right. Continue straight ahead along the grassy track. If you have reached a rightward bend in the track, you have gone too far. Opposite the path you want is a small gate set in the fence to your right.

6. Turn left at the post. Walk downhill along the narrower path, which has taken you away from the main track. Reaching a clearer area, where a way appears to join you from the left, walk straight ahead and keep going until you reach a point where there are tracks going to the right and to the left. Turn left and down. Emerge from the woods at the back of a row of cottages. Bear right down the lane to emerge opposite the car park in Blanchland.

14. Durham City

Distance: 2 miles.

How to get there: Durham City is well signposted from the A1(M) which bypasses it to the east. Vennels Café is in Saddlers Yard, which is a signposted vennel off Saddler Street, the street leading from the Market Place towards the Cathedral.

Start: The Market Place (GR NZ 276425), OS Pathfinder 572 Durham

The historic cathedral city of Durham is the backdrop for this short, but intricate, walk from the bustling Market Place, through the medieval streets and Norman cathedral to the tranquil College square and dramatic, wooded river banks.

Durham Cathedral

The Tea Shop

Vennels Café in Saddlers Yard is open from 9am to 5pm daily, including Sundays – it is closed only on Christmas Day and New Year's Day. Special sandwiches include avocado and smoked bacon, chicken with grapes and fresh tarragon, Wensleydale cheese and plum chutney. Scones are fresh-baked. Slices and meringues are all also baked in Vennels' own bakery, on the premises. The cake selection, which may feature carrot cake, chocolate cake, raspberry meringue, lemon slice, banoffee pie and coconut flapjack, changes daily and is written-up on the blackboard. There is seating for 50 people outside in the enclosed 16th century courtyard. The interior, on two floors, is equally authentic, resplendent with beams, nooks and crannies as a late-Medieval building ought to be, but complemented by modern design and idiosyncratic ex-sewing machine tables. Tel: 0191 3860484.

The Walk

The walk provides a tour of the city on foot and can easily be turned into a full day by touring the Cathedral, and maybe the Castle, more extensively, and taking advantage of the riverside leisure opportunities – including the famous Browns' boats for hire from Elvet Bridge and the more recent pleasure boat passenger trips. On the walk, the terrain is a mixture of pavements and unsurfaced riverbank woodland paths. There is a steep flight of steps at Kingsgate Bridge.

1. Start from the Market Place, at the two statues.

The statues here are of Neptune with his trident and of the 3" Marquis of Londonderry on his horse. The Marquis used to be an important coal-owner in the area around Durham. Look in the horse's mouth. There is no tongue. It is said that the realisation of this flaw in his otherwise perfect statue caused the sculptor to take his own life.

2. Orientate yourselves so that St Nicholas's church is behind you. Take the slightly leftward road – Saddler Street – out of the Market Place and walk up to the fork. Bear right into the street known as the Bailey. Walk up to the next fork and bear right along Owengate to the Palace Green.

Arriving at Palace Green, look for a frieze on the facing wall of the Cathedral, near the Rose Window end, which depicts the Dun Cow legend. Monks from the Abbey at Lindisfarne were transporting St Cuthbert's body in search of a final resting-place when they met a woman with a Dun (greyish-brown) cow. She pointed out this site and, when they wheeled their cart over to it, its wheels jammed. The monks took this to be a sign that they had found the spot to bury Cuthbert, and so they did. The present Cathedral was built on the site by the Normans and had its 900th anniversary in 1993.

3. Continue straight ahead, the Cathedral to your left.

Over to the right is the bastion of Durham Castle. It and the Cathedral were built on a steep rocky peninsula, nearly surrounded by the River Wear, because it was an easily defended site. The main danger was regular raiding of the North of England by the Scots. Nowadays, the castle is used as Durham University College.

4. Enter the Cathedral via the main door, with its Sanctuary Knocker.

The lion's head is the Sanctuary Knocker. In the Middle Ages, people running away from the forces of the crown could claim safety, or sanctuary, in the Cathedral by knocking at the door. The authorities were not allowed to enter the Cathedral, so the fugitive would be safe – while inside the Cathedral, at least!

5. Inside the Cathedral, walk across the main aisle to the glazed wooden doors. Pass through into the Cloisters.

You may want to take time out to explore the Cathedral. You will find the information desk as you enter the building.

6. You enter the Cloisters at the diagonally opposite corner from your exit. So, pick your route, and walk along two sides of the square to that opposite corner, where a tunnel leads you through to the open square known as the College.

Immediately on your right is the small memorial garden of the

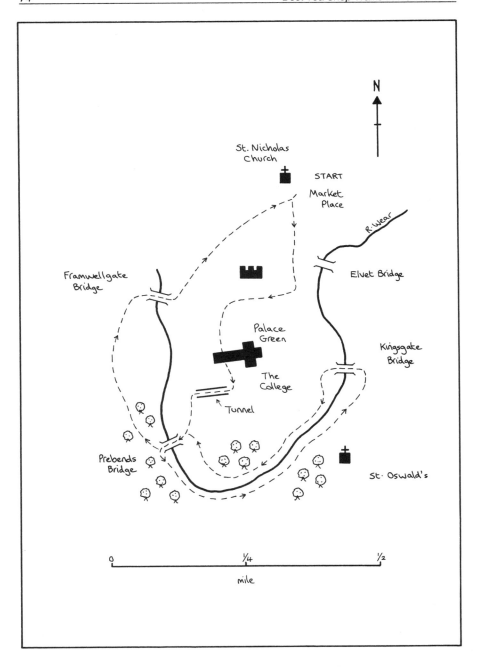

Durham Light Infantry (DLI). Around the square are the coats of arms of various Prince Bishops of Durham. There is a framed key in the arch round the corner to your left. Children may enjoy spotting some of these shields. The College is a pleasantly quiet square to while away a few minutes before continuing.

7. Exit the College via the tunnel which is to your right when you first enter from the Cathedral. The gate here is open until at least 6pm — later in the summer (until 10pm in June). Pause at the top of the path beyond the tunnel, looking over the wall, you can see a weir on the Wear! Next to it is a building that used to be a mill.

8. Turn left down the ramp. Keep going straight down to Prebends Bridge. Turn right and cross the bridge.

A potential **short-cut** here is to turn left instead, through the arch and walk down the Bailey to the Market Place, via the end of the cobbled lane to Kingsgate Bridge. At the far end of Prebends Bridge is a plaque with a poem by Sir Walter Scott.

9. Having crossed the bridge, turn left.

Another possible **short-cut** here is to turn right instead. You are now picking up the end of this walk, so follow the last few directions to the Market Place.

10. On the main route, follow the lower riverbank path around the outer bank of the meander.

The river is in quite a steep gorge here. This is called an incised meander. After the Ice Age, the land sprang back up from the relief of having the weight of ice removed. The River Wear was able to cut into this so that its bend, or mender, became steeply incised (cut) into the rock. The last advance of the ice was at its greatest extent approximately 18 000 years ago. However, the ice has advanced and retreated over Britain on numerous occasions (up to 20 in the last 2 million years), so it does not follow that the Wear's meander was incised in such a short period as 18 000 years.

11. As you round the meander, the path will lead you up towards the tower of St Oswald's church. Keep to it, ignoring minor distractions – particularly to the right, and walk through the churchyard to the war memorial cross.

On the left of the cross is a rosemary bush. Have a smell!

12. Keep walking and you will join Church Street. Follow the pavement down hill a little to round the bend. Turn left here, next to the concrete Dunelm House (Durham Students Union, DSU) to cross Kingsgate Bridge.

Looking ahead to the Cathedral from here you can see a large, round, stained-glass window, called the Rose Window. Each of the petals is a pane depicting one of the apostles.

Concrete Kingsgate Bridge itself dates from 1963. Its construction was in two separate halves – each initially parallel to the river which were then swung round to meet. Halfway across you can spot the join!

Possible **short-cut 3**, avoiding the many steps down to the riverside: at the end of the bridge, climb 17 steps and walk the length of the cobbled street ahead. Turn right and make your way down the Bailey to the Market Place.

13. For the main route, turn left at the end of the bridge, and descend the long flight of steps to the riverside. There are 103 steps.

14. Turn right at the bottom and follow the towpath right round the inner bank of the meander, past the colonnaded ruin of Count's House to a fork. Bear right and pass the tree sculpture on your left until you reach and re-cross Prebends Bridge. This time, turn right at the end and take the upper (left-hand) riverbank path from the obelisk.

Along here are classic views of Durham Cathedral.

15. The path leads you to a metalled lane. Turn right and follow this lane down to a junction just past the City Library. Turn right and right again to cross Framwellgate Bridge. Walk up Silver Street to the Market Place.

15. Stanhope

Distance: 2¼ miles.

How to get there: Stanhope lies astride the main A689 Bishop Auckland to Alston road. The Durham Dales Centre is in the town centre and is well signposted.

Start: Dales Centre Tea Room, Stanhope. NY995393 (OS Outdoor Leisure Map 31, Teesdale).

The Durham Dales Centre is an interesting combination of tourist service facility and local enterprise centre. As well as the tea room, there is the tourist information centre, craft workshops (some of which are open to the public) and a craft shop. It also serves as a business support centre, seeking to encourage economic regeneration in the Durham Dales.

Stanhope parish church

Stanhope itself is regarded as the capital of Weardale. The size of the parish church is testament to this standing and reflects the rich ecclesiastical living of past rectors – several of whom went on to become Bishops of Durham. The Market Place no longer has an active market function though its 15th century cross stands memorial to the past. The past goes a long way back in Stanhope, A 3000-year-old Bronze Age hoard of jewels and tools found here is now in the British Museum.

The Tea Shop

The Durham Dales Centre tea room has home-made fare served at the counter in a large, light, airy room which is further enhanced by murals of local scenes produced by artists from the area. Soup, including home-made thick vegetable and lentil, and hot dishes are alternatives to the tea-room's own scones, tea breads, cakes and pastries including home-baked fruit pies as well as crumble and sticky toffee puddings. There are jams and curds, country and flower wines and pottery on sale in the tea shop too. Most of the seats are inside, but there are some bench seats outside in the Dales Centre courtyard garden.

The tea room is open year round from 10am to 4pm Monday to Friday (to 5pm between April and October). Weekend opening is from 10.30 Saturday – half an hour later on Sunday – through to 4pm. Parking is at the Dales Centre and is free, although a box for voluntary donations is provided. Tel: 01388 527650.

The Walk

Beginning along the main street of this small dales town, the walk crosses fields to take you along the pretty little valley of Shittlehope Burn and later through the streets of upper Stanhope to return to the Durham Dales Centre via the Market Place and imposing parish church.

1. Emerging from the Dales Centre, turn left along the main street past the parish church and the complete length of the row of shops.

Front Street will become East End – apt street names for this linear settlement confined as it is to the narrow floor or Weardale and stretched along the Alston road.

2. Virtually at the end of Stanhope turn left into Woodcroft Gardens and then right onto the public footpath between the second and third bungalows. Cross the stile into a pasture and walk straight on, drystone wall to your left. At the far end is a small footbridge accessed by a gate. Cross the bridge.

This is Shittlehope Burn – a minor tributary of the River Wear. The first part of the walk is along its narrow and prettily wooded valley.

3. Turn left between a pair of stone gateposts to follow the stream side path, contrary to the flow of the stream. Keep walking. Negotiate a wooden stile on the way to a second footbridge. Cross this.

On the way a few narrow fishermen's treads branch off from the main path. Keep to the wider path each time, including one occasion when you will need to climb up a little over a few stones and slightly away from the stream-side.

There are occasional seats along here. If the first seems a little damp to sit on, persevere to the second.

4. Having crossed the footbridge, take the short flight of steps upward and at the top of the rise, turn right across a stile into a field. Bear left towards an already visible ladder stile and cross this to enter a larger field at its corner.

Ahead of you the view is across to the other side of Weardale.

5. Bear left along the field edge. There are trees on your left. When they and their enclosing drystone wall come to an end, look across the field at the drystone wall opposite. There is a ladder stile. Walk across to it, and cross over.

Depending on season and consequent height of crop growth, an alternative to the above is to bear right from the first ladder stile, along the top edge of the field and then alongside the drystone wall to the second stile.

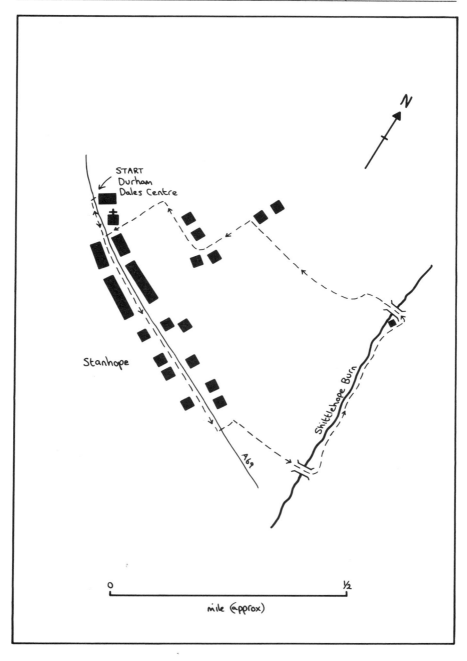

N

START
Durham
Dales Centre

Stanhope

Skittlehope Burn

A69

0   ½

mile (approx)

6. In any event, having crossed the latter stile, walk straight ahead, drystone wall to your left, until you reach a stone stile in the corner of the field. Negotiate this and continue straight ahead, again with drystone walling on your left.

The roofs of linear Stanhope, nestled in the valley, are now clearly visible down to your left.

7. At the next field corner is a further stile to cross before following the line of the wood and wire fence on your left to the field corner. Cross the wooden stile there, beneath the boughs of a sycamore tree, and walk along the short passage to a metal bar stile. Cross this too and turn left down the metalled lane.

8. As the metalled lane swings right, a fork heads downhill to the left. Don't be tempted. Walk straight ahead, at the same level.

Now back in Stanhope, this is High Street – another apt name. In this case it is high as in high up the dale side, rather than in the usual sense of being the main shopping street. The terraced streets of this quarter are reminders that Stanhope was once the centre of a lead and iron mining and smelting industry. During the Industrial Revolution the Stanhope and Tyne Railway fed the ironworks at Consett with locally quarried Pennine limestone.

9. Keep walking along, passing rather than descending Graham Street on your left, but keep a look out for the parish church and turn left down the lane immediately before the churchyard. At the bottom is the Market Place. Turn right and return to the Dales Centre.

Set in the wall of the churchyard, fronting the Market Place, is a curious fossil tree stump dating from some 250 million years ago.

16. Washington

Distance: 2½ miles or 3 miles or 4½ miles.

How to get there: Washington Wildfowl Park is well signposted within Washington – it is in District 15. Washington itself lies betwixt the A1(M) and A19 highways, between Chester-le-Street and Sunderland and is signposted from both roads.

Start: The car park adjacent to Washington Wildfowl Park (NZ 331563), OS Pathfinder 562 Washington and Chester-le-Street.

The Wildfowl Park (tel: 0191 4165454) is open 9.30am to 5pm, except Christmas Eve and Day. It and this walk are at the north-eastern end of the James Steep Park – a country park extending for about 3 miles along the banks of the River Wear named after Sir James Steel who was chair of Washington Development Corporation from 1964 to 1977.

Washington is proud to be "The original Washington" from whence George Washington's forbear emigrated to what became the United States. Modern day Washington is a New Town constructed around pre-existing mining settlements of which Washington was one. Planned in the 1960s as a car for the motor age, the New Town had an urban structure of broad highways linking intended " village" communities – themselves separated from each other by mini-green belts. Notoriously the signing policy has been by numbered district rather than "village" name. The Wildfowl Park is found by following signs "District 15".

The Tea Shop

Inside the Peter Scott Centre at Washington Wildfowl Park is the tea shop. The café opens at 10am and closes half an hour before the Centre – at 4.30pm in the winter and 5pm in the summer. There are home-made cakes, scones, cookies and afternoon tea specials. There is outside deck seating and views over the Wildfowl Centre lake. Local cuisine is recognised with Pitman's stotties and butties, corned beef and onion hotpot, Alnwick stew and a special "Taste of the North" dish of Wensleydale cheese complimented by date and orange chutney, home-made coleslaw and stotty bread served with a side salad. Tel: 0191 4165454.

The Walk

The walk begins from the car park adjacent to the Washington Wildfowl Park. The route described in detail here assumes you will also wish to pay a visit to the Wildfowl Centre and wander around its grounds on their shorter circuit. There is an admission charge. Outside the park my route is mostly on woodland, riverside or unsurfaced country path taking you on a pleasant stroll along part of the Wear Valley Trail with good views of Penshaw Monument.

Two extension options are easily added if you wish. Firstly, inside the Wildfowl Centre there is a longer waymarked circuit you could follow down to the riverside. Secondly, the High Wood Circular Walk adds a waymarked extra loop to the route fully described here.

1. Walk back out of the car park to the motor entrance. Turn right along the waymarked public bridlepath towards Low Barmston Farm. Walk along until you approach gates and a wire fence on the boundary of the Wildfowl Park. Bear left of these along the waymarked bridleway.

Washington Wildfowl Centre is run by the Wetlands and Wildfowl Trust. It has a collection of over 1200 swans, ducks and geese and a flock of Chilean pink flamingoes. Stock varies as the seasons unfold as there are large numbers of migrating birds who are transient residents. The Wildfowl Park is the third largest in Europe.

2. Walk along the unsurfaced path, past a wooden hurdle/baffle.

Over to the right is Penshaw Monument. This acropolis-style folly was built by local landowners to celebrate the legend of the Lambton Worm. This mythical creature was, according to legend, slain by Crusader Sir John Lambton from home the current Lord Lambton is descended. Worm is taken to mean dragon. At any rate the folk ballad of "The Lambton Worm" re-

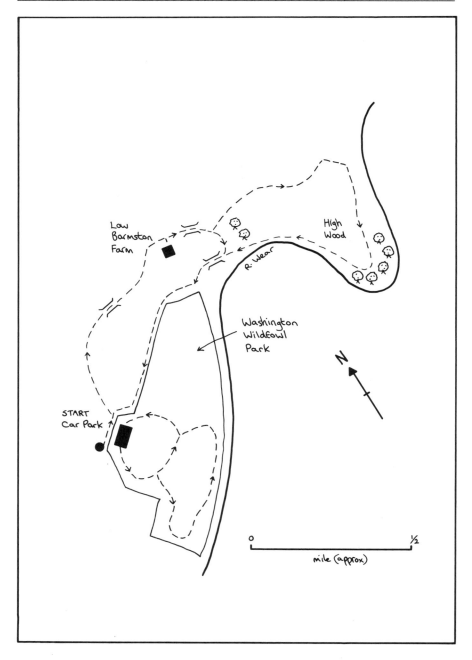

fers to it lapping its tail nine times round Penshaw Hill.. It is a moot point as to whether part of the folly of Penshaw Monument is that Worm Hill is nearby. However, the hill of the monument makes for a better landmark site and Penshaw Monument is certainly that — visible over much of north-eastern Durham and beyond.

3. Follow the path through pleasant, young woodland including beech, oak and sycamore, as well as the odd conifer, until the dolomite-covered way bends noticeably left.

A waymark post stands at this divide in the way. To the left is the path to Low Barmston Farm and down to the right, steps lead to a plank bridge over the stream in the direction of North Hylton. This is part of the Wear Valley Trail and is the way you will return at the end of the walk.

4. Bear left to follow the main, level, dolomite path. Keep going, sweeping right over quite a broad wooden footbridge and continue along the upper edge of a paddock. Carry on along the slightly narrower unsurfaced path, hedgerow to the left and fenced woodland to the right. Ahead is a stone-built house.

This is Low Barmston Farmhouse.

5. The path emerges opposite the gateway to the house's grounds. Turn initially left and then immediately right along the waymarked public footpath beside the outbuilding. There is a stile to cross. The path is signposted to the riverside. Follow it along and down to the right over two short flights of steps in quick succession to a beckside stile. Turn right, cross the stile and follow the path into the woods. Cross the footbridge you reach and follow the waymarking until you come to a waymark post opposite a stile on your left. This is indicated "High Wood Circular Walk".

A possible extension to the route described here is to turn left, over the stile, and follow this waymarked extra loop. It will add approximately 2 miles to your walk and takes you alongside the fenceline on your right as far as Wood House. There you turn right and walk down into High Wood to follow the path around the inner bend of the incised meander of the River Wear to rejoin the main route at the footbridge referred to in direction 6.

6. On the main route, continue straight ahead to the next divide in the ways. To the left is the way to North Hylton, but you should take the right-hand fork in the direction of Washington. Descend the steps to the footbridge. Cross it and follow the riverside path.

Here is a good view and photo opportunity of Penshaw Monument over the Wear.

7. Ascend the flight of steps to which the path leads, away from the river and up to a fenced farmstead. Follow the waymarking leftward, walking alongside the enclosed Wildfowl Park on your left. This path brings you to the plank bridge over the stream referred to earlier (after Direction 3). Cross this little bridge and ascend the steps, bearing left to retrace your earlier steps back to the car park.

17. Killhope Wheel

Distance: 3½ miles.

How to get there: Killhope Lead Mining Centre is in upper Weardale, right next to the A689 Stanhope to Alston Road, 2½ miles west of Cowshill.

Start: Killhope Lead Mining Centre Car Park, NY825432 (OS Outdoor Leisure Map 31, Teesdale).

The Killhope Lead Mining Centre aims to bring to life the harsh times and circumstances of the people who worked here in Victorian times. The Wheel itself rotates and the surface buildings and mine yard have been restored to give a picture of how life would have been here in the 1870s. There is an optional guided mine tour (not available for under 4s), for which advance booking is advised at peak times (tel: 0191 383 3337). The Centre charges admission (£3.40 per adult, rising to £5 to include a visit down the Park Level Mine, though with the usual concessions for age, disability and employment status). It is open daily from 10.30am to 5pm between April and October, and on Sundays only (10.30 to 4.00) in the period from November to March. There is no need to pay the charge to go on the walk but the tea shop (the Killhope Kitchen) is inside the centre.

The Tea Shop

The Killhope Kitchen forms an integral part of the Killhope Wheel Lead Mining Centre and is located within its main building. Scones are home-baked daily and cream cakes may include Pavlova. In fine weather there is outdoor patio seating; on more inclement days, hot fare including filled baked potatoes may be more welcome. Tel: 01388 537505.

Killhope mining centre

The Walk

Killhope is in the North Pennines – "England's Last Wilderness". Bear this in mind. Parts of this walk reach an altitude of 550m and some sections are open moorland exposed to the elements. You will need to be equipped for windy, wet eventualities. The route follows a sweeping arc through the Weardale Forest, returning via moorland track and rough pasture path.

1. Between the Welcome sign and the Centre, turn right along the waymarked public footpath next to the bus stop and walk up to and then cross the stile adjacent to a farm gate to enter coniferous woodland.

This is part of the Weardale Forest – a working forest. Some public rights of way deviate from their routes as depicted on the Ordnance Survey map, but are waymarked on the ground. Directions given here may also vary temporarily – be guided by forest waymarking should this occur.

2. Follow the gravelly track, ignoring another which branches off to the left, until eventually the whole track swings upward to the left to clear the trees. Follow the indicated public footpath further left and walk along with the coniferous trees on your left.

The body of water now on your left is Kidd's Dam, constructed as part of the 19ᵗ century lead mining operations at Killhope. Such dams would hold back water allowing it to be released downstream at rates to suit the water wheels and mills below.

3. From the end of Kidd's Dam continue to follow the main gravel track up to and over the crest of the rise. Continue walking, the forest on your left, until you reach a point where the gravelled track curves left downhill, but the signposted public footpath leads you straight on ahead. Initially quite muddy, this route soon becomes a narrow path with occasional wooden causeways.

4. Keep the forest edge on your left as you follow its gentle curve round to the left. Emerging into more open country, you will see a wooden stile ahead. Walk up to it and cross to head right along

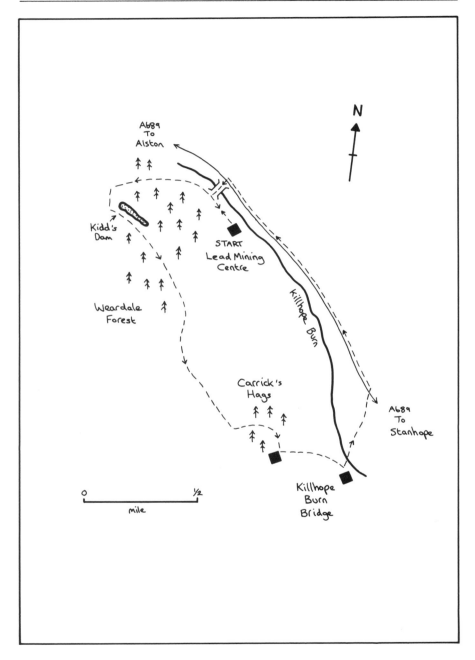

the causeway to the next stile. Cross this and turn hard left by a wood and wire fence.

The view of Weardale from here is of dispersed farmsteads set on the gentler slopes and interspersed by patches of coniferous plantation.

5. At a corner a waymark arrow causes you to bear left. Keep the wood and wire fence on your left as you descend the bank-side. At the bottom of the bank is a field corner and a waymarked stile indicates a left turn.

On the day I walked this route this section had been temporarily diverted. The waymarked diversion is described.

6. At the next fence corner the waymarking takes us right onto a gravel track. Very soon a waymark post is reached. Ignore it and continue straight on along the gravel track until you reach a T-junction. Turn left and walk up to the gate access of the plantation. Enter the woods of Carrick's Hags and continue.

7. Arriving at a stone built house, turn right to cross the cattle grid and walk, slightly downhill, along the track. Pass the end of the track leading left to isolated High Byre and carry on until you reach a T-junction of ways.

The confluence here is of Wellhope and Killhope Burns. Over to the left is an abandoned farmstead at Killhopeburn Bridge. Mining has ceased and hill sheep farming is very marginal. The landscape of upper Weardale is therefore littered by old, semi-ruined stone structures of various sorts.

8. Turn left and walk down to the ruin at Killhopeburn Bridge. Cross the old bridge and then head left, across the face of the abandoned building, to the cattle grid. Pass through the adjacent gate.

This is a public footpath. Any private road notice is only to deter vehicular traffic.

9. Walk to the end of the short stretch of drystone wall where there is a Weardale Way marker. This directs you up a grassy path to ascend the bank. Keep going until you reach a waymark post directing you slightly left. Making for the line of telegraph poles ahead, pass the abandoned quarry on your right, on your way to pass through a small blue sheep gate set in drystone wall. Walk down the dip and then head right to the waymarked gate. Reaching the metalled main road, head left to return to the Lead Mining Centre.

18. Fir Tree

Distance: 3½ miles.

How to get there: Fir Tree is on the A68, 1 mile south of the roundabout junction with the A689 Crook to Wolsingham road.

Start: From the Old School House (NZ 139345, OS Pathfinder map no. 580) and begin by walking towards the central corner junction, turning right and continuing alongside the A68 until you are almost opposite the petrol station.

Fir Tree is a hamlet on the main A68 Darlington-Corbridge road, 2 miles south-west of Crook. Nowadays it retains a road-side service function. There are three inns and a petrol station, as well as the tea shop. The junction on which it stands is relatively minor but the bend in the road has the effect of slowing passing traffic and implanting an image of the place on the traveller – good for business!

The Old School House Tea Room

The Tea Shop

The Old School House Antiques and Tea Room is alongside the A68 in Fir Tree, a little to the north of the main corner in the direction of Corbridge. The tea shop opens on Fridays and Saturdays from 11am to 5pm, and on Sunday from 1pm to 5.30pm. It is closed for the month of October and on Bank Holiday Mondays. Home baking, afternoon tea and antiques make an interesting end-of-walk combination. The Old School House was a church as well as school in its time. Although no children have been taught here since in the 1920s, there are old photographs of the time on view. There are speciality teas to enjoy and a daily selection of home-made cakes, tarts and slices, as well as sandwiches, scones, teabread and a set afternoon tea. Tel: 01388 765699/766919.

The Walk

A walk over the fields for the most part, passing rustic, seemingly quite isolated farms, away from surfaced roads. Part of the walk takes in a section of the Weardale Way. The route is without any very steep slopes. Fir Tree is on the main A68 and a short stretch beside this is inevitable, though minimised.

1. Turn right onto the waymarked public bridleway across the stile. Walk down the concrete driveway, passing through a wooden farm gate into Hollin Hall wood. Continue along the concrete drive until you approach metal-railings.

2. Turn right, off the concrete drive, onto a narrow earth path. Walk down into the dip. You arrive at a right-angled corner in the fence line. To the right is a stile to ignore. Straight on is the stile you want to cross. Do so — it is next to a white metal gate — and turn left to walk down the edge of the pasture.

   Some of this pasture is not especially well-drained and the going can be a little squelchy along here. You will also encounter a ditch, which you can step over if you choose your spot.

3. At the bottom of the pasture is a waymarked stile. Cross and bear right along the track towards the farm at Wadley. At Wadley, bear

right again to join the main farm drive, which crosses the front of the farm. Walk along, past the farm-house and adjacent cottage.

This is part of the Weardale Way. This is a long distance foot-path running the complete length of the River Wear — right down to Sunderland. It is rather more then than just a way through Weardale. This next section of the walk, as far as New Plantation, beyond Harperley Hall, is part of the Weardale Way.

4. To the right of a pair of hen houses you will find two green metal gates at right angles to each other. Pass through the gate straight in front of you and carry on along the right-hand side of the pasture. There is a thorn hedge on your right.

5. Arriving at the woodland edge, cross the stile and follow the path down to the right.

Improvement work to this section of the Weardale Way has been carried out by the Durham Volunteer Rangers with the support of both the Countryside Commission and Durham County Council. The path is in part stepped.

6. Cross the wooden footbridge to ascend the steps on the other side. Follow the path as it bends right between the trees and leads you to a waymarked stile to cross into a pasture field. Cross this field by walking initially straight up to the crown. From here you can see a wood and wire fence leading down from the level of the now visible Harperley Hall. In the fence is a stile. Make for it.

7. Cross the stile and walk straight on over the open pasture towards a white gate.

Harperley Hall, has clearly seen better days. Rather isolated, without a paved drive for instance, its enclosed grounds were surrounded by open, parkland style landscaping to allow the owners to enjoy a pastoral surrounding to their more formal gardens. Originally pioneered in the 18ᵗ century by landscape designers such as Capability Brown, this style of estate plan-ning typifies many of the large houses and halls of England.

8. Reaching the white gate, pass through and continue straight

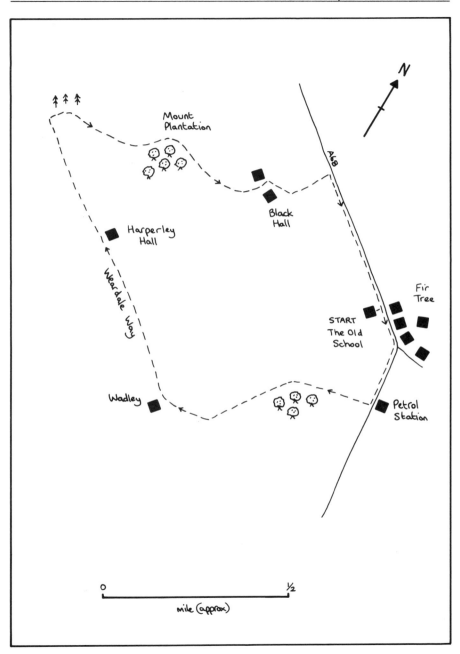

N

Mount
Plantation

Black
Hall

A68

Harperley
Hall

Weardale Way

Fir
Tree

START
The Old
School

Wadley

Petrol
Station

0   ½
mile (approx)

ahead along the stone and grass track along the top edge of New Plantation. At the next gateway, cross the stile and then turn right up the track to a further waymarked gate. Pass through.

You have now left the Weardale Way.

9. Walk along the track, to the side of the crop field, bearing right at the angled corner, as the track does. Then swing left to the next waymarked gate and stile combination. Negotiate this and follow the line of the wood and wire fence on your right as it skirts around the edge of Mount Plantation.

10. Pass through the two gates you encounter in quick succession, on either side of a narrow, windbreak, band of trees. Follow the track to a metal gate just ahead of the next farm — Black Hall. Pass through this gate, but ignore a pair on your right which give access to a metalled lane. Instead follow the unsurfaced track as it sweeps left just before the first house to lead you between that and a cow byre to your left.

Notice the interesting weather vane standing in the garden of the house.

11. Turn right, beyond the blue metal gate, to walk the length of the farmyard and then follow the drive ahead as it curves left. Follow this bridleway up to the main road and turn right to follow the vergeside path back to Fir Tree.

19. Eggleston

Distance: 7 miles.

How to get there: Gatehouse Farm, Eggleston is on the B6278 Barnard Castle to Middleton in Teesdale road. This is the high road, above the valley. An alternate route is the B6277 from Barnard Castle, turning right to Eggleston at Romaldkirk and driving uphill from Eggleston Bridge to Gatehouse Farm.

Start: Gatehouse Tea Room, Gatehouse Farm. (OS Outdoor Leisure Map 31, Teesdale) NZ 003236.

The village of Eggleston has a couple of pubs, a post office and a shop – enough to satisfy the requirements of this small commumity. Depending on when you visit the village, you can enjoy the fair in August or the Eggleston Show in September – a very typically rural event with cattle, sheep and local produce all on show.

The Tea Shop

The Gatehouse Tea Room was once the toll house for Eggleston. This farmhouse tea shop is open from ten o'clock in the morning until late in the evening. There is the opportunity to sit outside in fine weather. Speciality teas include Cream Tea and a full Afternoon Tea with sandwiches, scone and cake. Puddings on offer include home-made apple pie. Dogs are welcome and there is accommodation for smokers and non-smokers alike. Tel: 01833 650830.

The Walk

From Gatehouse Farm, the walk heads down to cross the Tees at Eggleston Bridge from which a circular route extends mostly over fields to Romaldkirk and beyond via part of the Teesdale Way above the banks of the river. If the full route is a little daunting, a shorter stroll to and from Romaldkirk, perhaps with a visit to Eggleston Hall Gardens thrown in, may be an alternative worth considering.

1. From the tea-room walk alongside the main road down the hill to the junction. Bear left in the direction of Romaldkirk, Mickleton and Eggleston Hall Gardens.

The entrance to Eggleston Hall Gardens (tel: 01833 650403) is on the right. You might like to visit them now or after your walk. They are long-established walled gardens with a great variety of species to view and are open daily (except Christmas Day) from 10am to 5pm.

2. Pass beneath the double arches which span the road and carry on to cross Eggleston Bridge before turning left onto the waymarked public footpath.

This is the first bridging point for motor traffic upstream of Barnard Castle. The path is waymarked "Teesdale Way" — a long distance footpath along the Tees, part of which you will be following on this walk.

3. Beyond the gate, follow the path ahead. It is easily picked out as a flatter, greener ledge in the otherwise steeper pasture. Rise up to a corner and follow the wood and wire fence on your left. This fence becomes a wall and guides you to a waymarked stile.

4. Cross the stile. Follow the main Teesdale Way path straight ahead. This deviates from the line of the wall, which begins to drift away to your left.

A minor path head off to the right from the stile. Ignore this for the moment, although you will find yourself returning along it from Romaldkirk later.

5. Head across the rough pasture towards a telegraph pole on the skyline. Beyond, continue to follow the path to the corner of the field where there is waymarked signpost. Follow the path down to the right towards Romaldkirk village.

6. Walk along the path a little to the left of the field boundary towards the corner of woodland ahead. Reaching this you will find a waymarked stile to cross into the woods. Follow the path. There is now a low drystone wall to your right.

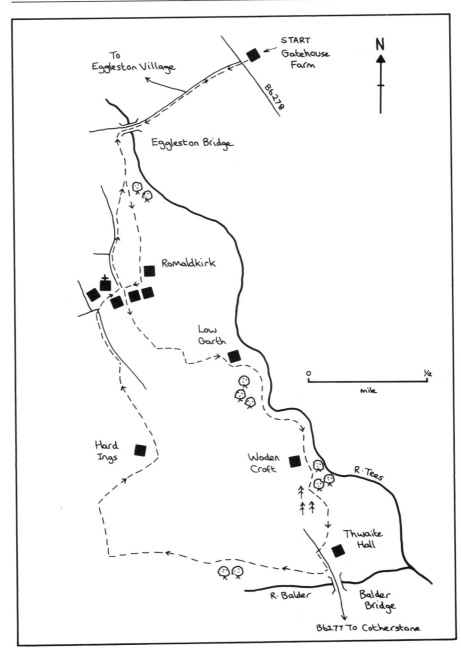

7. Cross the small, single slab stone footbridge you encounter on your way to the woodland edge where you emerge into a high-hedged narrow lane which lead to the end of Romaldkirk village green. Turn right to walk along as far as the Kirk Inn and then turn left across the face of this establishment and make for the waymarked continuation of the Teesdale Way ahead.

You may want to pause a while in Romaldkirk. This is a pretty Teesdale village formed by a number of stone-built houses surrounding a large and quite open village green. St Romald's church is unusually large for such a small place and is nicknamed the "cathedral of the dale" in consequence. There are two pubs – the Kirk Inn serving food and real ale and the Rose and Crown. The latter is a hotel as well as serving meals in its restaurant and in the cosy bar where there is a fire. Again, real ales are on offer.

The Rose and Crown, Romaldkirk

8. Join the waymarked public footpath straight ahead. Use this to leave the green, between the stone cottages. Keep going to a waymarked gate. Pass through into a pasture.

The majestic trees here are beeches.

9. Walk straight ahead to the last beech tree and then bear left to the top of the field's central mound. From here a single waymarked gate is visible. Walk down and through it, to diagonally cross the next field to pass through another gate and then head downhill towards a farmstead.

The buildings ahead of us are Low Garth. The banks of the River Tees are just beyond.

10. At Low Garth, cross the stile beside the metal gate and turn left across the front of the farmhouse. Follow the grass path as it skirts the edge of the field to a waymarked stile in the bottom corner. Cross into the woods.

Look down to the Tees on your left. You should be able to see some rapids.

11. Walk on. Cross the next stile and the stream immediately beyond it. Continue until you walk across a flat piece of ground on the inside of a river meander. Here a lane develops. Walk up to cross the stile at the top and then to pass through the succeeding gate before following the fence on your left that leads you on to the next habitation.

The set of buildings you are now approaching is called Woden Croft.

12. At Woden Croft, pass along the lane to the left of the barn, through two gates, and then along the front of a row of cottages to a white metal gate. Pass through.

13. Your route is to the right – after passing through the gate. At the corner of the pasture a waymark arrow will direct you through a farm gate into some woods. Cross the beck, ignoring the isolated footbridge and walk up the other side to the next gate. Pass through and carry straight on along the field edge until you cross a waymarked stone stile into the grounds of Thwaite Hall. Walk along the drive to the road.

14. Turn left to walk as far as the bridge to Cotherstone village (the Balder Bridge). Turn right just before the road crosses the bridge.

Alternatively, carry on to Cotherstone itself. The Fox and Hounds pub in Cotherstone is on the opposite side of the bridge and may be an appropriate refreshment stop. As pubs go, it is a little up-market. There is another pub and a Post Office general store further along the village street. On leaving the village, to return to the route, one of the last buildings on the right (Balder View) has an unusual fox-shaped weather vane.

15. On the main route, descent the steps and bear right across the pasture and up a rise to the fenceline. Follow this, to pass through a gate onto a gravel lane.

The elegant stone house on the right is Dow Park.

16. Pass through the next two gates and cross the succeeding stile. Walk straight across the field and pass through the next gate and cross the stile following that. However, ignore a further stile you may notice on your left, and continue to follow the fence round the edge of the field until you pass through a gap at the end of a hedgerow. You need to look out for a gate on the left along here.

17. At the gate, bear right to cross a waymarked stile. Walk on. Cross the pair of ladder stiles, either side of the cutting, to walk across the pasture beyond to a red metal farm gate. Pass through and turn right along the stony track. Follow this, rounding a rightward sweep, until you join a metalled lane, through a green gate. Turn right onto the lane and walk along until you come to a house on the left. This house is called Hard Ings.

18. Turn left onto the track beside the house . Cross the next stile onto a lane that brings you through a gap in the hedgerow and eventually to a gate. Pass through, past a small stone store, and down to the field corner. Turn left and walk up to the stile on your right. Cross it and walk to the crest of the field. From here walk ahead to a gate and beyond that, cut the corner of the next pasture to another gate. Pass through and walk over to the concrete barn on your left. Follow the painted arrows to pass the house there and walk down the lane to the road. Turn left and walk back to Romaldkirk.

19. Walk across the Green to the church and follow the metalled lane out of the village to the right of the churchyard. At the junction bear right and walk along to a public footpath way marker on your right, after rounding a leftward curve in the lane.

20. At the waymarker turn right and pass through the gap stile. Follow the path across pasture to a stone stile to the right of a silvery metal gate. Having negotiated this, walk straight on to the stile next to the wall ahead. Turn left to cross this and retrace your early steps back to Gatehouse Farm.

20. Middleton in Teesdale

Distance: 5½ miles.

How to get there: The direct route from Barnard Castle is to take the B6278 to Eggleston and continue on to Middleton. Alternatively, the B6377 via Cotherstone meanders through several pretty, stone-built villages en-route to Middleton from "Barney".

Start: car park in the main square, NY 947255 (OS Outdoor Leisure Map 31 Teesdale).

The ornate drinking fountain in the main square was erected on September 28th 1877 by Mr Robert Bainbridge of Middleton House in commemoration of a testimonial given to him by the workers of the London Lead Company. Middleton was then the centre of a thriving lead mining industry in Teesdale and Mr Bainbridge was the Superintendent.

Country Style Bakery

The Tea Shop

The Country Style Bakery and Tea Shop in Market Place is open from 9am to 5pm, Monday to Saturday and from 10.30 to 5pm on Sundays from mid-March to mid-December. Afternoon and cream teas are available and specialities include rich cheesecake and rum truffle cake. The tea shop is non-smoking, has disabled access and welcomes well be-haved dogs.

Other options in Middleton include the Chatterbox in Chapel Row and the Teesdale Hotel in Market Place. This last has some out-side seating on its courtyard terrace. Tel: Country Style Tea Shop, 01833 640924, The Chatterbox, 01833 640789, Teesdale Hotel, 01833 640264.

The Walk

The walk begins in the centre of Middleton in Teesdale, crosses the Tees and continues along field paths for the most part, although some sections are along metalled lanes. At around 5½ miles, it is a little longer than some others in this book and includes a significant climb at Intake Hill, followed by some open moorland

1. Walk down to the river, that is to say in the direction signposted Scotch Corner, B6277, towards Mickleton. Cross the bridge over the Tees and walk on until you pass the Cattle Mart on the right. Turn right along the public footpath, waymarked Pennine Way.

This is the first of a couple of short stretches of Pennine Way taken in by this walk. The acorn logo is instantly recognisable.

2. Walk up to the stile, cross it, and continue along the track ahead, passing through a gate and crossing a further stile on your way to a small bridge over a stream. Cross the bridge and begin to follow the main track beyond, past a stone barn and wooden farm gate set in a drystone wall on your right, to the top of a little rise. Be-neath the boughs of an ash tree is a divide in the way.

3. Bear left, away from the main Pennine Way and the line of the drystone wall, between the stream to your left and the line of tele-graph poles on your right. Walk along until a drystone wall crosses your way. To the right of a water gate is a stile to cross into a succeeding pasture. Continue, keeping the stream to your left.

Along here, on your left, a cement slab farm bridge crosses the stream to a farm gate. Ignore it.

4. Cross the next stile you reach, again to the right of a water gate, into sheep pasture and walk along with the drystone wall now on your left. Make for a gap in the drystone wall on the opposite side. Pass through and continue walking until you reach a wooden footbridge crossing the stream.

5. Cross the footbridge and make directly across the narrow pasture for a wooden gate. Negotiate this and turn left onto the metalled lane. Walk along the lane for about three-quarters of a mile.

This quiet lane is the minor road to the settlement of Holwick and nowhere else. Holwick is a hamlet of stone-built cottages and farms, with a single pub – the Strathmore Arms.

6. · Almost the end of the lane, opposite a pair of cottages, the Pennine Way is clearly waymarked. Bear right and walk up to and through the gate.

To short-cut the walk at this point, continue to the end of the lane and then turn left to walk down to the bridge over the Tees and back to Middleton in Teesdale.

7. Beyond the gate, walk along and up the gravel track until you reach the crest of the rise. Here a farm track crosses your way from left to right, but you continue straight on along the stony track.

You are climbing Intake Hill. In hill sheep farming terminology, intake is land from the valley side (rather than floor) which has been enclosed and to some degree improved for grazing. The rougher, open grazing land of higher up the fell will be reached after the climb. Pause occasionally to admire the view back over the valley.

8. Carry on walking until you reach and pass through a metal gate. Beyond the gate is open grazing land and the Pennine Way sweeps around to the right. However, you press straight on, uphill, over the crest to rejoin the clearer farmer's track. Carry on along this track, uphill, towards the next break of slope. From there a metal gate set in a wood-and-wire fence becomes your goal.

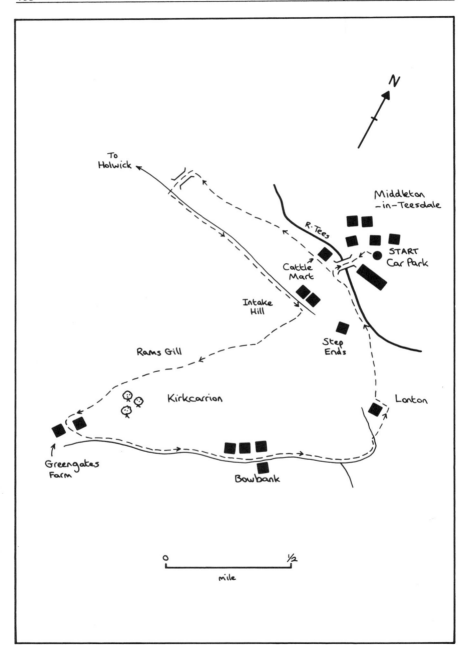

9. On gaining the gate, cross the adjacent stile and continue to follow the track ahead and up.

On the left here are abandoned workings – the disused Middleton Quarry.

10 Keep following the green sward way, now joined by another path merging in from the left. Swinging right, you will appear to be walking to the tree-topped summit ahead.

In fact the route sweeps around the base of the summit mound of Kirk Carrion – a barrow – along the line of Rams Gill – a minor dry valley.

11 The path approaches a gate very closely, but you veer right and follow the green path as it circumnavigates the summit and eventually approaches a drystone wall on the other side of Kirk Carrion. Parallel this, walking with the wall on your left. Look out for a stile on your left. Cross it, over the wall, and walk through the small depression you enter, veering right towards stone ruins when these become visible.

Hill farming is, and has for some decades, been a marginal economic activity. Together with the decline of mining and quarrying, this accounts for the frequency of abandoned and ruined buildings in the higher parts of the dales of the Northern Pennines.

12. As you approach the round stone wall, you will pick up a green track leading off to the left. Follow it to a viewpoint.

The valley before you is Lunedale – a tributary to Teesdale. The reservoir is Grassholme Reservoir.

13. Follow the path downhill, to the right. At the bottom, swing left through a green gate.

Appropriately this is Greengates Farm. There are several green gates to be seen. The road here is from Middleton in Teesdale to Brough, about 13 miles away.

14. Make your way between the farm buildings to the road and turn left alongside it. Follow the road for 1¼ miles in total, passing through pretty Bowbank, en-route to a road junction where a minor road branches off right towards Mickleton, Romaldkirk and Barnard Castle. Continue along the relatively main road to round a left bend.

15. Once you have cleared the bend, look for a public footpath sign on the right. Turn onto this field path, via a stone gap stile and a short flight of steps, into a pasture field. Bear left towards the ladder stile you can see at the bottom. This will turn out to be the first of a pair on either side of the route of the dismantled railway.

16. Beyond the second stile, bear slightly left through the gap between the farm to your left and the gentrified dwelling to the right. Ahead of you is a road, which you access via a gap stile. Turn left onto the road—albeit briefly. Then turn right, as waymarked, over a stile onto another field path. Bear left across the pasture along the trodden path to the succeeding stile. Cross this too and bear right towards the trees beyond the drystone wall and a small gap stile. Go through and follow the path down, bearing left to make towards a further stile in the far corner of the narrow strip of pasture.

17. Cross this stile too and follow the farm track ahead, the River Tees now on your right. Pass the farmstead of Step Ends on your left and keep going along the track to join the road opposite the Cattle Mart. You have come full circle. Turn right and return to Middleton.

21. Yarm on Tees

Distance: 4 miles.

How to get there: Yarm is on the A67 Crathorne to Darlington road and is signposted from the A19 trunk road. Strickland and Holt is a small-town department store on the High Street beside the Town Hall. There is parking on the High Street cobbles as well as behind Stricklands.

Start: Strickland and Holt, High Street (NZ 419128, OS Leisure Map 26, North York Moors, West or Pathfinder 601).

Yarm is on the banks of the River Tees, south of Middlesborough and about a 45 minute drive from Newcastle upon Tyne. Its history dates from the 12th century and it was at one time the main port on the Tees. Its importance as a port declined with the development of Middlesborough, but Yarm is still a busy small town, with an attractive and bustling main street.

The Tea Shop

The Restaurant inside Strickland and Holt is on the first floor. It is an open, loft-style room with table service, although it is a good idea to walk up to the counter and view the tempting cake selection, including hazelnut and lemon meringues, ginger grundy and banoffie pie as well as home-made ice cream, before ordering. Scones are made to their own recipe, with sultanas, date or cheese. A range of teas, including a specially blended Yorkshire is available. Opening hours are simply 9am to 5pm, Monday to Saturday. Tel: 01642 791234.

The Walk

From cobbled Yarm High Street the walk will take you through some of the backways of old Yarm and along the banks of the Tees, through hidden, bijou Egglescliffe village back to Yarm. Out of town, much of the route is on field paths. Although the majority is level,

Egglescliffe village green

some of the cross-country stretch can be very sticky and muddy. You will need to be prepared for this.

1. From the front entrance of Strickland and Holt cross the High Street by the Town Hall.

Yarm has had a long history of floods. On the Town Hall wall are several heights of flood plaques. The flood of September 1771 was clearly impressive. There is also, among several further plaques, one commemorating the five railway pioneers who met in Yarm to agree to build the world's first locomotive-hauled passenger railway from Stockton to Darlington in 1825.

2. Having crossed the High Street, walk right and few paces only and then turn left down the cobbled High Church Wynd – sign-posted Stockton Railway Heritage Trail. Emerge onto West Street.

The house on the corner – Hope House – is Elizabethan and

thought to be the oldest in Yarm. West Street does indeed lie west of the High Street, which it parallels.

3. Cross West Street and turn left down the lane to the left of Crofton House. This path is again signposted "Stockton Railway Heritage Trail" and leads to the riverbank. Turn right to walk along the surfaced path by the Tees – "True Lovers' Walk".

Further downstream, below Stockton, is the Tees Barrage. Since this was finished in 1994, the Tees above it has no longer been tidal. You will notice the flood gauge where you join the riverside path, but the flood risk is intended to be lessened now. There are wooden platforms built out from the bank for the use of anglers.

4. Continue to walk along the river path, passing the church on your left, and rounding the meander.

Yarm is built within the loop of a meander of the Tees – a factor in its flooding problem. Dating back to Roman Times (Iarum), it was for centuries the lowest bridging point, and main port, on the Tees. Stockton, and certainly industrial Middlesbrough, are more recent usurpers of that role.

5. Keep walking past the viaduct

The viaduct was built by the long-gone Leeds and Northern Railway Company in 1849. A total of 43 arches straddle not just the Tees but much of old Yarm, the length of the High Street, though slightly to its west. It includes 7 million bricks. Through the arches you will see Egglescliffe parish church which you will be passing near the end of this walk.

6. Immediately beyond the viaduct, the path splits. Take the upper option.

The houses to the right have two gates each. The conventional garden gate has behind it a heavy-duty burgundy-coloured flood gate.

7. Walk on as far as, but not beneath, the stone road bridge.

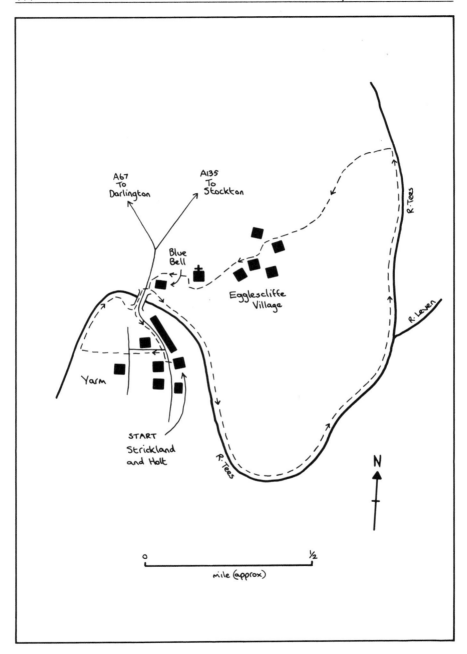

This ancient bridge has clearly had many of its stones replaced over the century, nevertheless still included within it
are stones laid by Bishop Skirlaw (of Durham) in 1400. The
Tees at Yarm was for centuries the boundary between County
Durham to the north and the North Riding of Yorkshire to the
south. Yarm was thus the first/last town in Yorkshire. Since
the creation of County Cleveland in the 1970s this boundary no
longer exists – at least constitutionally. Yarm is part of the
modern borough of Stockton on Tees. Among locals, however,
there are those for whom the river still plays its traditional
role.

8. Turn right along the snicket to emerge at the end of Bridge Street.
Turn 180° left to cross the bridge.

On the wall of the shop opposite the snicket there is still a
white rose plaque announcing the North Riding of Yorkshire.
Half-way over the bridge the old boundary is indicated by a
plate set in the wall of the central bay on the downstream side.
CD is County Durham.

9. Cross the road as well as the bridge so as to follow the curving
stone wall, on the northern bank, to the right towards the Blue Bell
riverside pub. Turn right down the waymarked steps to follow the
public footpath through the beer garden.

This is actually part of the long-distance footpath – the Teesdale Way. The stile you are approaching is carved with the mes-
sage "Sail to the Sea" on the side facing you and "Swim to the
Source" on the opposite side. On the opposite bank of the river
you will be able to see the post-barrage boardwalk pier from
which river cruises now run.

10. Cross the stile and follow the main river bank path for a total of 2
miles. There are few field boundaries to cross along here – the
odd stile and a couple of kissing gates well round the meander.

Buildings on the opposite bank begin with modern riverside
apartments, giving way to the substantive Friarage building
which is the core of independent Yarm School. Further on mod-

ern detached houses have gardens dipping down to personal boat landings on the river. You may also notice the confluence of the rivers Tees and Leven,

11 Opposite the slightly off-white White House Farm, is a rather impressive metal waymark post erect by Egglescliffe Parish Council to mark the 1994 centenary of parish councils. Turn left, away from the river, up the field edge path in the direction of Egglescliffe.

From the top of the rise here you can see over to the Cleveland Hills on a clear day. The new housing development of Ingleby Barwick lies between you and the pyramidal hill of Roseberry Topping , which stands above the general skyline of the Cleveland Hills. To its right you may be lucky enough to pick out the obelisk of Captain Cook's Monument.

12. Cross the waymarked (River Tees Valley) stile you encounter beside a pylon. Cross its immediate successor into a field and walk along the pasture-edge path as afar as a farmyard on your left. Waymarking here is confusing. Turn left to cross the stile into the farmyard and then bear right to exit, past a public footpath sign, onto a metalled lane. Walk straight ahead until the whole lane bears left of a brick wall.

On the right here is a waymarked public footpath. Ignore it.

13. Bear left to the secluded and very pretty Egglescliffe village green. Walk straight on to the old-style public telephone box and then head right, down Church Road. Pass the tiny Pot and Glass pub on your left and follow the path straight ahead. Skirt the churchyard of Egglescliffe parish church on the right and emerge at the war memorial.

14. Bear left down the surfaced path, through the cycle baffles, to emerge by the Blue Bell pub. Cross the bridge back to Yarm High Street. Walk up the High Street to the Town Hall and Strickland and Holt.

Tea Shop Walks — Spreading everywhere!

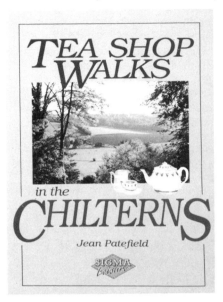

The Sigma Leisure Tea Shop Walks series already includes:

Cheshire

The Chilterns

The Cotswolds

The Lake District, Volume 1

The Lake District, Volume 2

Lancashire

Leicestershire & Rutland

North Devon

The Peak District

Shropshire

Snowdonia

South Devon

Staffordshire

Surrey & Sussex

Warwickshire

The Yorkshire Dales

Each book costs £6.95 and contains an average of 25 excellent walks: far better value than any other competitor!